TWAYNE'S WORLD AUTHORS SERIES

A Survey of the World's Literature

Sylvia E. Bowman, Indiana University

GENERAL EDITOR

INDIA

Mohan L. Sharma, Slippery Rock State College

EDITOR

Bhabani Bhattacharya

TWAS 343

Bhabani Bhattacharya

Bhabani Bhattacharya

By DOROTHY BLAIR SHIMER
University of Hawaii

TWAYNE PUBLISHERS
A DIVISION OF G. K. HALL & CO., BOSTON

Library of Congress Cataloging in Publication Data

Shimer, Dorothy Blair.
  Bhabani Bhattacharya.

  (Twayne's world authors series, TWAS 343. India)
  Bibliography: p. 137–46.
  1. Bhattacharya, Bhabani—Criticism and interpretation.

PR9499.3.B45Z88   823   74-19219

ISBN 0-8057-2151-7

891
B575S

MANUFACTURED IN THE UNITED STATES OF AMERICA

Contents

About the Author

Dorothy Blair Shimer is an Assistant Professor in the English Department at the University of Hawaii, where she teaches courses in World Literature and Oriental Literature. A graduate of Skidmore College with a master's degree from Bread Loaf School of English, Middlebury College, she has also done graduate study at Exeter College, Oxford University, and at Syracuse and Columbia Universities.

Her acquaintance with India, and with a dozen other countries of Asia, developed into an abiding love and appreciation of Oriental cultures and literatures. For four years (1954–58) she and her husband lived and worked with people of cities and villages from Japan and the Philippines to India, Pakistan, and Iran in a non-governmental program for education in intergroup relations. Since that time there have been visits for personal enjoyment and exploration.

Professor Shimer's *Mentor Book of Modern Asian Literature* (1969) and *Voices of Modern Asia* (1973) are paperback anthologies recognized as probably the only comprehensive collections of modern Asian literature in English translation. Her articles and reviews appear regularly in literary and professional journals in the United States and Asia.

Preface

As one of India's foremost writers of fiction, Bhabani Bhattacharya merits a study of his life and work. Evidence that he is an increasingly recognized figure may be seen in the fact that scholars of India and the West are now researching his writings as bases for doctoral dissertations or scholarly papers and the Boston University Library has acquired his publications and papers for its Special Collections archives.

Bhattacharya, however, is more than an Indian writer of note. Since he uses an international language—English—as his medium, from the moment of his first published novel he entered the world scene. *So Many Hungers!* was brought out almost simultaneously by leading publishers in Bombay and in London. Subsequently his books have originated from Crown Publishers, New York, and have moved rapidly into the stream of world literature through translations into twenty or more languages. It is interesting to note that as a writer in English Bhattacharya is undoubtedly more widely known in his own country than he would be if he had confined himself to Bengali, his mother tongue, or to Hindi, the national language. He points out that translations into the languages and dialects of India go more readily from English than from the regional media.

Because of Bhattacharya's use of English, his English education, and the theme of East-West accommodation that runs throughout his writing, it seemed fitting to present first a brief background of the presence of the Western powers in India ("Between Two Worlds").

Following the Chronology and the introductory chapters, the major works are taken in order of publication, each providing title for a separate study. Since forms other than the novel may be seen as of secondary interest to Bhattacharya, and therefore to us, his essays and short stories are considered together ("Essayist and

Teller of Tales"), and other miscellaneous works are grouped ("Translator/Editor/Biographer").

Consideration of the novels in chronological sequence seems not only convenient but logical. Bhattacharya has set each of his novels against the backdrop of an historical event or period, thereby giving a sense of sequence in time—from the World War II days of *So Many Hungers!*, *Music for Mohini*, and *He Who Rides a Tiger*, through the post-war Independence period of *A Goddess Named Gold*, to the 1962 confrontation of China and India across the vale of Ladakh.

There is a sense of chronology, also, in Bhattacharya's development as a writer and thinker. From the first published work, *So Many Hungers!* to *Shadow from Ladakh*, there is evidence of increasing mastery of technique. It is interesting, in addition, to note successive variations on the themes of heroic struggle against hunger and social injustice, adjustment to changing times and mores, and the building of bridges of understanding between cultures and nations, between social groups, and between individuals at all levels. Bhattacharya, the historian and political scientist, is sensitive to time and change.

This study cannot, of course, be considered final. Indeed, one of the challenges to the writer during the past two or more years has been the need for continuous updating of material and thinking, for Bhabani Bhattacharya continues to be active as a creative writer. I have been fortunate in being able to talk many times—often for long periods—with him and his wife, Salila, during their years in Honolulu and, since then, to keep up a stream of correspondence between Hawaii and St. Louis, Missouri, where the Bhattacharyas now live with their son and his wife.

DOROTHY BLAIR SHIMER

University of Hawaii

Acknowledgments

Acknowledgment should first go to Bhabani and Salila Bhattacharya for their unlimited generosity in giving time for long conversations, in responding graciously to questions, and in sharing reviews, news items, and letters from their personal files. Thanks are also due the novelist himself for permission to quote from his published works.

Howard B. Gotlieb, Associate Director of Libraries for Special Collections, Mugar Memorial Library, Boston University, provided a major portion of the information needed for the list of Bhattacharya's published works. The bibliography of German translations of stories came largely from a meticulous itemization by Erica Kalmer, London, who has served as agent as well as translator for the German market.

Appreciation is expressed to the National Book Trust, India, for permission to quote from the volume *Gandhi the Writer: The Image as it Grew*, to the Sahitya Akademi, New Delhi, for similar clearance for the quotations from *Rabindranath Tagore, 1861–1961: A Centenary Volume*, as well as to the following for use of passages from their publications: Taplinger Publishing Company, New York, and Sidgwick & Jackson Ltd., London, extracts from *British India* by Michael Edwardes; the Indian Council for Cultural Relations, New Delhi, quotations from *India and Southeast Asia: Proceedings of Seminar on India and Southeast Asia*; *The New York Times*, excerpts from "Shall I Paint Myself White?" by Dom Moraes; W. W. Norton Company, Inc., William Morris Agency, New York, quotations from Nayantara Sahgal's "From Fear Set Free"; and the *Quarterly of South Asian Literature* (formerly titled *Mahfil*) for quotations from a review and a Bhattacharya interview.

Individuals who have been helpful are Dr. B. B. Agarwal, Assistant Secretary of the Sahitya Akademi (National Academy of Letters), New Delhi, who furnished a copy of Bhattacharya's award citation from the Academy; Millen Brand, editor of the Bhattacharya novels, Crown Publishers, New York, some of whose comments are quoted here; and Dr. Everett Kleinjans, Chancellor of the East-West Center, Honolulu, who shared his impressions of the author as a Senior Specialist at the Center and who provided a copy of Bhattacharya's project proposal for his year at the Center as well as a copy of the paper presented on the occasion of Dr. Harlan Cleveland's inauguration as President of the University of Hawaii. Brief quotation has been made from both documents.

I was stimulated by corresponding and talking with Professor Marlene Fisher of Manhattanville College, New York, and reading her critical articles on Bhattacharya's work, several of which look with discernment into the novelist's masterful depiction of the female psyche. Thanks are also due B. Syamala Rao, Lecturer at the S.K.B.R. College, Amalapuram, India, for a copy of his article on Bhattacharya as a novelist, published in *Triveni*, Madras; to Dr. K. R. Chandrasekharan, Director of the Language Institute, Gujarat University, Ahmedabad, for assistance with the bibliographical references for a number of Indian sources; and to the Institute for Comparative and Foreign Area Studies, University of Washington, Seattle, for copies of materials resulting from Dr. Bhattacharya's visiting lectureship there.

Special, personal acknowledgments should be made to my husband, whose helpful criticism and editorial experience helped to see the manuscript into final form, and to the University of Hawaii, for providing a teaching reduction to facilitate completion of the writing, and a financial grant to cover the costs of manuscript typing, which was accomplished with special finesse by student Linda Todt.

Chronology

1906   Bhabani Bhattacharya born November 10 of Bengali parents at Bhagalpur, Bihar State, northeast India.

1920   Begins to write for *Mouchak* in Bengali.

1923   Enters Patna College at Patna, the State capital. Begins contributing to India's leading Bengali and English periodicals. Wins literary awards.

1927   Takes the Bachelor of Arts degree with Honors in English Literature and begins work toward the Masters.

1928   In September, sails from Bombay for England to study at the University of London.

1929   Begins to contribute to British periodicals. Translates prose sketches and poems of Rabindranath Tagore, most of which appear in *The Spectator*. Meets Tagore, then travelling in Europe.

1930   Tagore translations appear in book form under the title, *The Golden Boat* (in London and New York). Travels extensively in Europe. Contributes to *The Hindu* (Madras) a biweekly feature, "In London Today," and a series of articles, "Europe—Behind the Veil."

1931   Receives Bachelor of Arts degree with Honors in History, University of London. Returns to India for three-month summer vacation. November, meets Mahatma Gandhi for the first time, in London.

1931–   Extensive travel throughout Europe.
1933

1934   June, awarded Doctor of Philosophy degree in History, University of London. In December, returns to India and settles in Calcutta.

1935   Marries Salila Mukerji, daughter of Dr. D. M. Mukerji and Ushamoyee Mukerji of Nagpur. Begins to contribute a biweekly feature to *The Statesman* (Calcutta); also, a weekly feature to *The Hindu* (Madras).

1936   With wife, visits Rabindranath Tagore at Santiniketan.

1937   Settles in Nagpur. Son Arjun is born.

1941   *Some Memorable Yesterdays* published in Patna.

1943   Plans to write a novel based on the happenings of that war-time year in India. In December, daughter Ujjaini is born.

1947   Daughter Indrani born in February. *So Many Hungers!* published in October in Bombay.

1948   *So Many Hungers!* published in London and becomes a selection of the prestigious Left Book Club in England. *Indian Cavalcade* published in Bombay.

1949   Russian translation of *So Many Hungers!*, published in Moscow.

1949–   With family goes to Washington, D. C., to serve as Press
1950   Attaché, Embassy of India. Article on Prime Minister Jawaharlal Nehru syndicated in the American press. First ten chapters of *Music for Mohini* serialized in the *Illustrated Weekly of India*.

1950   Czech translation of *So Many Hungers!*, published in Prague.

1950–   Three-year contract as Assistant Editor, *Illustrated Weekly*
1952   *of India*, Bombay. Leaves before contract period ends.

1951   Slovak translation of *So Many Hungers!*, published in Bratislavia. Member of first Indian Cultural Delegation to the U.S.S.R., invited by the Union of Soviet Writers. Commissioned by *Letteraturnaya Gazetta* (Moscow) to do an article on "How I Wrote *So Many Hungers!*" Travels 20,000 miles in the Soviet Union. Stops in Prague, Rome, and Paris on return journey. Polish translation of *So Many Hungers!*, published in Warsaw.

1952   *Music for Mohini* published in New York. *Mohini* selected by Le Club Français du Livre, a leading book club in Paris, and appears in French translation.

1953   Swedish translation of *So Many Hungers!*, published in Stockholm. Selected to be a member of the Advisory Board for English of the newly formed Sahitya Akademi (National Academy of Letters).

1954   *He Who Rides a Tiger* published in New York. *So Many Hungers!* published in German in Berlin.

1955   Chinese Writers Union, Peking, brings out *So Many Hungers!* translated into Chinese from the Russian. Russian translation of *He Who Rides a Tiger* serialized in magazine *Inostrannaya Literatura*, Moscow. Publication in book form follows. Polish translation of *He Who Rides a Tiger*, published in Warsaw. Italian edition of *Music for Mohini*, published in Turin. Paperback edition of *He Who Rides a Tiger* (Bombay). Delegate to Asian Writers' Conference in New Delhi.

1956   Danish translation of *He Who Rides a Tiger*, published in Copenhagen. French translation published in Paris. "The Crocodile Pool" appears in a Polish anthology, *Adjanta*, Warsaw. Receives invitation from Moscow University to participate in an international seminar; accepts, but is unable to attend because of ill health.

1957   *He Who Rides a Tiger* published in Serbo-Croatian (Yugoslav), German, Finnish, Sinhalese, and Spanish translations. The Sinhalese is serialized in the periodical, *Silomina*, while an English version is partly serialized in *Jana*, both issued in Colombo. The Spanish translation is by the South American novelist Miguel Angel Asturias, Buenos Aires, who becomes 1967 Nobel Prize winner in literature. *He Who Rides a Tiger* appears in serial form in *The Sunday Standard*, Bombay. Receives offer from Peking for Chinese translation rights to that novel.

1958   Slovak, Chinese, and East German editions of *He Who Rides a Tiger* published. "The Cartman and the Steel Hawk" included in an Australian anthology, *Span*, Melbourne. Attends with wife Salila the World Congress on Intellectual Cooperation in Stockholm.

1959   *He Who Rides a Tiger* published in Czech translation in Prague. *Music for Mohini* appears in British edition (London). Accepts appointment as Executive Secretary of the Tagore Commemorative Volume Society (Chairman: India's Minister of Education) and Chief Editor of a selection of Tagore essays. Delegate to a two-month International Seminar at Harvard University (Executive Secretary:

Dr. Henry Kissinger; Coordinator: Alan Tate). Meets Millen Brand, his editor at Crown Publishers. "A Moment of Eternity" appears in an anthology, *Contemporary Indian Short Stories*, published by Sahitya Akademi.

1960   Delegate to three-week Harvard-Japan International Seminar, Tokyo, followed by tour of Japan under escort of Dr. Henry Kissinger. Wife Salila accompanies. "The Crocodile Pool" anthologized in *Following the Sun: Seventeen Tales from Australia, India, South Africa* (Berlin). *A Goddess Named Gold* published in New York. *He Who Rides a Tiger* put out in a British edition (London). Spanish version of *A Goddess Named Gold* published in Barcelona.

1961   Delegate to Tagore International Seminar in New Delhi, sponsored by UNESCO. *Towards Universal Man* published in Bombay. Contributes "Tagore as a Novelist" to *Rabindranath Tagore, 1861–1961: A Centenary Volume. A Goddess Named Gold* serialized in the *Illustrated Weekly of India.* "A Handful of Figs" included in a German anthology (Frankfurt).

1962   German translation of *A Goddess Named Gold* becomes a quarterly selection of the foremost book club in Germany. Accompanied by wife, goes to New Zealand to receive "Prestige Award" from the Universities of New Zealand, and makes lecture tour of university centers. Extensive tour of Australia as official guests of the government. Attend the Adelaide Festival of Arts. Contract from India's Ministry of Education to be Literary Editor of the *Gazetteers of India.*

1963   Author and wife visit West Germany as guests of the government. At Frankfurt meets the Dutch publisher, Adrian Stok, and is drawn into a warm friendship. Stok accepts for Dutch publication *A Goddess Named Gold* and *Music for Mohini.* Visit London as guests of the British Council. Polish translation of *Music for Mohini* issued in Warsaw.

1964   Publication of *He Who Rides a Tiger* in Hungarian: *Aki Tigrison Lovagol.* Begins writing *Shadow from Ladakh.*

1965   *Music for Mohini* comes out in Russian translation (Moscow). Hebrew translation of *A Goddess Named Gold* published in Tel Aviv.

1966   Delegate at international seminar on Southeast Asia, New Delhi. Boston University establishes the "Bhabani Bhattacharya Collection" in its Special Collections archives. Receives a research grant from the Asia Foundation. Publication of *Shadow from Ladakh* (New York). Publication of *One Hundred and One Poems by Rabindranath Tagore*.

1967   Publication of British edition of *Shadow from Ladakh* (London). Edits series 11 of *Contemporary Indian Short Stories* (Sahitya Akademi, New Delhi). "A Moment of Eternity" included in *Razkazi Ot Mnogo Meridiana* ("Short Stories from Many Meridians") published in Sofia. Invited to be Senior Fellow at the Institute of Higher Studies, Simla. Withdraws acceptance following heart attack.

1968   Accepts grant from Ford Foundation to write a centennial volume on Mahatma Gandhi. *Shadow from Ladakh* receives the Sahitya Akademi Award. *Steel Hawk and Other Stories* published as a Hind Pocket Book (Delhi). "A Bridge Between the Peoples" appears in *India and Southeast Asia: Proceedings of a Seminar* (New Delhi).

1969   Receives a travel award from the Ford Foundation. Guest of the British Council in England. Meetings with British writers. Visits the Hague to meet Adrian Stok and wife Eva. Dutch version of *Shadow from Ladakh* follows. Publication of *Gandhi the Writer: The Image As It Grew* (New Delhi). Accepts a year's appointment as Senior Specialist, Institute of Advanced Projects, The East-West Center, Hawaii. Participates there in international Gandhi Seminar.

1970   Presents paper at "After Vietnam, What?" conference held on occasion of inauguration of Dr. Harlan Cleveland as President of the University of Hawaii. Writes for *Abbottempo* a commissioned article entitled "The Nature of Wisdom."

1971   Accepts year's appointment as Visiting Professor, University of Hawaii. Helps in University-sponsored Tagore Festival, which includes stage presentation of dance drama, *Chitrangada*, produced by wife Salila.

1972   Joins son and family in St. Louis, Missouri. Ill health prevents serious work.

1973   Several weeks as Walker-Ames Professor, University of Washington, Seattle, where he delivers a series of public lectures under the rubric "Asian Universalists": "Swami Vivekananda: A Bridge Over The Oceans," "Rabindranath Tagore: Lifelong Dynamism," and "Mahatma Gandhi: Brave New Thoughtways." Also presents a paper, "Images of Women in My Stories," at an inter-university conference. Widely hosted and honored. On invitation, visits University of British Columbia, Vancouver, and delivers public lecture, "Re-introducing Tagore."

1974 –   Begins writing first novel outside the Indian setting—*A*
1975   *Dream in Hawaii.*

CHAPTER 1

Between Two Worlds

I *The Colonial Scene*

THE child born to Promotho and Kiranbala Bhattacharya in Bihar, India, on a wind-scuffed November day in 1906 may not have had the appearance of the typical British subject. But British subject he was, nonetheless. For English rule had established the "Indian Empire" close to half a century earlier, and its capital then in Calcutta, was only a pulse beat away.

As the son of a well-to-do judge of the Brahmin caste, the boy was heir to the cultural riches of two worlds. It is ironic, but undoubtedly true, that the heritage more readily accessible was that spawned half a world away on alien islands lashed by salty seas, so different from sun-bathed Bihar through which flowed the sacred Ganges.

We might remind ourselves of some of the developments that introduced Western cultural exoterica to the sub-continent and nurtured the seedlings to the extent that indigenous growth was virtually crowded out, especially in educational and urban centers.

Europeans had become increasingly involved in the life of the sub-continent since Vasco da Gama, the great Portuguese explorer first entered, in 1498, the harbor of Calicut, on the southeast coast, after a voyage of ten months from Lisbon—a distance spanned in hours today. The Dutch, French, and English followed hard in the wake of those early ships. When the English East India Company came in 1600, under a charter granted by Queen Elizabeth for trade in pepper and other spices, the small group of private entrepreneurs seemed an unlikely foundation for the powerful empire which would develop over the following three centuries. Riches other than spices were discovered in Hindustan—silk, cotton, gems, camphor, indigo, jute, tea, opium, sugar. But the greatest wealth of all was the unlimited supply of cheap and apparently willing labor.

1

By the eighteenth century the English traders had established a network of business and influence and eventually forced out the Dutch, containing the Portuguese within the 1500-square-mile Goa settlement on the west coast south of Bombay, and the French in an area one tenth that size, centered around the city of Pondicherry on the southeast coast below Madras.

Gradually the British crown became more involved in what had begun as a private trading venture enjoying no more than governmental sanction. Military commanders were sent to quell disturbances, many staying on to govern. The British remained in largely autonomous governing areas generally defined by geographical, linguistic, and cultural divisions set by Indian tradition. Assumption of unified power by the British Crown did not come until 1859 in the aftermath of a massive uprising of Indian soldiers ("sepoys") against their English superior officers.

II   *Westernization*

The ascendancy of the British Raj was accompanied by extensive cultural infusions. By the time of Bhabani Bhattacharya's birth the acculturation process had reached its apex. Western values, modes, art forms, had been heavily superimposed upon the native culture. In ninety per cent or more of the country Westernization was synonymous with Anglicization. Ironically, it was in culturally rich Bengal that English patterns, especially in education, were most highly prized. A British journalist-scholar writes:

In Bengal, government policy was to establish either an English or what was called an Anglo-Vernacular school—i.e. a school which used both English and the local language—at the headquarters of each administrative district. The best of these schools were given college status, and were linked with lower schools by a system of scholarships. Higher education was available at the Hindu College at Calcutta, which was finally taken over by the government in 1854 and renamed Presidency College.[1]

Rich and vital expression in the arts was also subordinated to British preferences. Michael Edwardes points out that "the first development of an art designed to suit British taste seems to have begun at Murshidabad, the former capital of Bengal."[2]

The ultimate in the ruler's sense of superiority to the people ruled may be found in a statement by John Lawrence, a high ranking official of the East India Company, who became an early Viceroy (1864–69) of the British Government in India: "We have not been elected or placed in power by the people, but we are here through our moral superiority, by the force of circumstances, by the will of Providence. . . ."[3]

In the cities and among Indians of the higher castes and professions, an education in the British pattern was accepted as a birthright. Among the wealthiest there were English tutors to instruct children in the home before they were sent abroad to English universities. Or there were the thoroughly Anglicized schools and colleges in India. Some young men who went to England to study became so British they left their Indianness behind and came, like writer Dom Moraes today, to ask "Shall I paint myself white?" In an essay of that title, Moraes says of his own case:

I am Indian by birth, but I have lived in England since I was a boy, and I hold a British passport. The historical accident of British rule in India worked on my family, so that I lived an English life there and spoke no Indian language. . . . So English was my outlook, I found I couldn't fit in India. When, eventually, I came to England, I fitted in at once.[4]

Nayantara Sahgal, niece of former Prime Minister Jawaharlal Nehru, however, views British culture as, actually, no more than a light crust covering the steaming life of the masses of the people:

In Northern India nearly every city developed along similar lines, its English crust, crisp and light and removable, atop a filling of Hindu and Islamic culture.

Below the crust level the filling had its own separate complex existence. . . . But all this went on below the crust. To the foreign observer, for the most part, the pie stood uncut on the table, only its puffy crust on view.[5]

Something of the trauma of the sensitive personality caught between two worlds was revealed by an Indian friend who once remarked somewhat bitterly that his first efforts in poetry were sonnets in praise of the hedgerose and the English thrush. It took years for him to recognize the poetic possibilities in the jasmine and the bul-bul bird.

As an aware, sensitive, and responsive personality, growing up in a family of Bengali culture, Brahmin caste, and professional class, Bhabani Bhattacharya would have reacted in much the same fashion to the two worlds—interrelated yet unrelated—in which he grew.

III *Independence*

Independence, after three centuries of foreign rule, finally tore back the crust of British culture to reveal the substantial mix that had all along been the sustenance of the people.

Bhattacharya was too young to feel any impact from World War I, in which his countrymen had supported the Allied cause with general enthusiasm. More than a million men served under the British standard. Contributions of money and materiel poured in.

Certain hard-core dissidents, however, latched upon the government's moment of weakness to build opposition to the colonial hierarchy and to engage in terrorist acts aimed at undermining colonial power. The dream of independence, which up to this time had been shared by a scattered few political activists, captured the imagination of social reformers and political leaders, British as well as Indian. A war fought in Europe on behalf of democracy could not but have an ideological impact on colonialized India. It was time for Great Britain to begin practicing in Asia the convictions her men were dying for in Europe.

At the close of the war, nearby Bengal became the center of increasing dissident activity. Political assassinations, bombings, and violent demonstrations at one extreme could be balanced at the other by the freedom songs of such poets of genius as Rabindranath Tagore, Divijendra Lal Roy, and Bankim Chandra Chatterjee, as also by the spiritual affirmations of Mohandas Gandhi, whose nonviolent resistance galvanized world sympathy. When hundreds of highly respected men and women of all castes, all social levels, and all provinces were thrown into prison as enemies of the Empire, the road to freedom was laid down. The ultimate destination was clear, only the timetable remained in doubt.

These were the political and social forces that swirled about Bhabani Bhattacharya as he left adolescence and reached manhood in Bihar. He would be a young graduate student in London when the famous Round Table Conferences were held there in the early 1930's—conferences seeking to achieve India's freedom without revolutionary violence.

Another world conflagration, moving from the European theater through Southeast Asia and threatening Bengal itself, would be lived through before the end of the freedom road was reached. And the way would, after all, be drenched in blood.

India felt the effects of World War II more directly than she had Great Britain's previous war involvements. Not only did she again provide a million fighting men and valuable war goods, but devastation moved into the homeland.

It was a cruel act of fate that, with manpower drained by the war effort and Japanese forces pressing hard against the corridors between Burma and Bengal, nature herself should turn against an already beleaguered people: famine followed in the wake of the failure of the Bengal rice crop in the winter of 1942–43. A gripping account of the agony of a starving people can be found in Bhattacharya's *So Many Hungers*! More than two million died in Bengal alone as a result of the great famine of 1943—almost ten times the number of Indian soldiers sacrificed in all of World War II.

But with death there was birth. As a result of promises made by the British Government during the course of the war, the independence of India was finalized July 18, 1947.

IV *Partition*

With the birth of free India there was also death. Gandhi, the British Viceroy for India, and others who were involved in the independence negotiations had vigorously opposed any agreement based on a sectioning of the sub-continent along geographic, linguistic, or religious lines. Eventually, however, Hindu-Muslim clashes killing several thousands forced recognition of a source of friction that could not be ignored. Reluctantly it was agreed that the only solution lay in the division of the country into two separate entities—India to include those areas with a predominantly Hindu population and Pakistan (*Pak*, "pure"; *stan*, "land"), those largely Muslim. Political expediency fractured geographical logic. Pakistan was subdivided into two wings: West Pakistan embracing the northwestern portion of the Punjab to the borders of Afghanistan, and East Pakistan the eastern two-thirds of the state of Bengal. More than a thousand miles of India, as well as basic differences in language and culture, lay between.

When the formalities were completed, not one but two new nations were born: the sovereign democratic republic of India and the Islamic republic of Pakistan.

Immediately there were mass migrations over the newly defined borders—Muslims hurrying to take up residence in Pakistan and Hindus in India. By the time some 6,000,000 Hindus and Sikhs had shifted to India and 6,500,000 Muslims to Pakistan, close to half a million lives had been taken in mutual slaughter. What was considered a historical "first" in recriminatory genocide would be matched in 1971 when East Pakistan tore itself loose from the uneasy alliance and formed the independent nation of Bangladesh.

V *Authentic Background for Fiction*

The Independence movement and its eventual success, the great Bengal famine of 1943, something of the impact of World War II, the traumatic effects of Western values and technology on India's deeply rooted culture, the move of China across the vale of Ladakh toward Bengal are all background elements in Bhattacharya's novels and stories. Social abuses in the name of the Hindu caste system also appear as motivating forces. Notably absent, however, are reflections of Hindu-Muslim tension and the cataclysmic events accompanying partition. When I asked Bhattacharya about this curious omission from the work of a socially aware writer, he replied that he and his family lived through those years in the shelter of Nagpur. The destructive forces set in motion by communal distrust, the carnage, seemed far removed from the comparative calm in the Central Provinces.

Interestingly, however, the tragedy in Bangladesh, which tore at the heart and soul of all the Bengali people, was too close, too severe an emotional experience—even from Hawaii, where he and his wife then lived. When asked if the events of 1970–71 would inspire his writing, Bhattacharya answered that they were too painful to live through in the author's creative process.

This is the background—formed of the basic materials of two cultures—against which Bhabani Bhattacharya writes.

CHAPTER 2

The Making of a Writer

I *Unlimited Horizons*

A MONG Bhabani's earliest memories are the "plump law books" that crowded his father's bookshelves, interspersed with works of great literature in Bengali and in English. The father, a civil servant at the time of his son's birth, later became a judge. Rich cultural influences at home had worked on the boy well before his formal schooling began at the age of six in the seaside town of Puri on the Bay of Bengal, where the family lived during several of his early years.

More than half a century later the sea with its unlimited horizons would still be etched deep in Bhattacharya's mind.

The major influence in those years was the sea itself. Puri beach is one of the most attractive in the world, almost furlong-wide stretches of bright sand extend for miles, enormous breakers crested with foam roaring down upon them. The most brilliant sunrises and sunsets. The sands sloped gradually into the salt water and bathing was an immense pleasure. Long canoes of the fisherfolk rode perilously over the breakers, but a furlong beyond, the sea was calm.[1]

He recalls that he spent most of his evenings lying on the sand and gazing across the vast expanse of ocean. This love of the sea would possess him all his life, and years later, during world-wide travels, he would take every opportunity to enjoy a sea view. He sought such vistas on both sides of the English Channel, on the French and Italian Riviera, the Norwegian shores, over the Gulf of Finland from Leningrad, across the limitless Pacific from Australia, New Zealand, and Hawaii.

Even in those early school years, when still not much more than a child, his creative response to literature would be discovered and nurtured.

7

At school I drew the attention of a scholarly teacher of Sanskrit, who had strong literary interests. He often took me on walks in the course of which he would cite a line of poetry and ask me (then in my early teens) to compose a rhyming line to make a couplet. I enjoyed the "pastime" and it did me good. I soon began to write poems that were not just couplets.

He was still at school when he began contributing poems and prose sketches to *Mouchak* ("Beehive"), the best children's magazine of the time. The periodical published the work of some of the topmost writers, including the great Rabindranath Tagore, who was to become a major influence in Bhattacharya's personal and creative life. His contact with *Mouchak* continued for many years.

The early reading was confined mainly to Bengali literature—poetry, fiction, drama—until, toward the close of his school days in India, he discovered Shakespeare. He recalls that he found the collected works in his father's library and "read every play."

Early in 1923 his pre-university schooling was completed. The award of a top scholarship was unexpected, he says, since he had given more time to reading omnivorously in response to his awakening literary interests than to the textbooks prescribed for examination needs. In the middle of that year he entered Patna University.

The adjustment to university life was not altogether easy, however, for, as he put it, he "entered through the wrong door."

I enrolled in the Science Department with Physics, Chemistry, and Mathematics as my subjects. I had romantic ideas about Science, and possibly dreamed of attaining greatness in that field. Disillusion came quickly when, in the laboratory, I began to play havoc with test tubes and apparatus. Finally, at the university examination the supervisor watched my predicament as I was trying to analyze the chemical composition of a mixture. To save my career he worked on the mixture and found the answer for me. All my instructors must have felt great relief when I moved to the Arts program where I belonged!

During the Patna years, he "fell under the spell" of Tagore's poetry. But new horizons were opened by some of the greatest writers of the West. Romain Rolland's *Jean Christophe* "overwhelmed" him, and Bernard Shaw began to influence him. There was also the invigorating literature of Norway—the works of Ibsen, Knut Hamsun, and Johan Bojer. A favorite American author at that time was Walt Whitman, who would be followed later by such socially aware writers of the twentieth century as John Steinbeck, Sinclair

Lewis, John Dos Passos, Upton Sinclair. And there would be Alan Paton, one of his favorites, whose books on Africa were, like his own, written "from a base of social concern."

II   *The Writer Emerges*

While still an undergraduate Bhattacharya wrote a series of articles on world literature for *Vichitra*, a leading Bengali magazine with which Tagore was associated. He also wrote a number of poems, mainly sonnets. ("At that time I yielded to poetic outbursts," he has said.) Fifty years later, his voice quivering with emotion, the world-renowned novelist would quote verbatim a brief note he received one day from the poet: "I like your work. Keep on writing. All my blessings." Said Bhattacharya, "For a student not yet out of his teens nothing more world-shaking could have happened!"

Heterogeneous influences that had converged upon boy and young man during the most impressionable years were coalesced by the Nobel Laureate's praise. No matter what occasional by-roads Bhattacharya's career might take in the years ahead, from this point on the central direction would inevitably be creative authorship.

With the beginning of Honors work in English Literature in his third year at Patna, Bhattacharya undertook his first writing in English. His short sketches and literary criticism appeared first in the college magazine and then in Sunday editions of Calcutta papers. Literary prizes and publishers' checks helped to set the direction of a young life.

The early adoration for Tagore continued (indeed, would persist throughout a lifetime), and it was inevitable that Bhattacharya's first translations from Bengali into English would be of Tagore's poems. These found publication in a literary magazine of Calcutta University.

It was at this time, at the age of nineteen, that the young Tagore enthusiast made his first "pilgrimage" to Santiniketan. Bhattacharya recalls:

The small colony of writers and scholars was built up by Tagore on a barren stretch of wasteland far from the crowded cities. Here, Tagore had established his school and later his World University of India (Visva-Bharati) which attracted great scholars from abroad. Tagore was perhaps the most approachable man among the great, but I was so dazed by the sight of him that I did not have the courage to meet with him face to face. I was content to be merged in an audience listening to his discourses, and also to absorb the atmosphere of the "hermitage," as Santiniketan was rightly called.

Somewhat later Bhattacharya won a prize in a literary competition organized to select Tagore's poems for an anthology, *Sanchaiyta*. That was the prelude to a personal relationship with the poet—a relationship that would deepen and mellow through the years.

III   *The English Experience*

When he had received his Bachelor's degree with honors in 1927, the young scholar-author was strongly encouraged by his father to continue his studies abroad. Bhattacharya's intention had been to continue his work in literature at King's College, University of London, but the professor to whom he was assigned gave him a cold reception. According to Bhattacharya the welcoming remarks concluded with the general indictment: "I don't understand why Indians want to come to this department. Their English is sickening."

Insulted and wounded, Bhattacharya made a decision that would have significant bearing on the course of his life and especially on the nature of his writing. He turned away from the English Department, but not from the University or London. Rather, he sought admission to the History Department. There he was received with warmth. "So," he says, "I bade goodbye to Literature and devoted myself to History which, to then, had been a secondary subject in my college courses." He adds that he never regretted the decision. Certainly, the decision should not have been regretted, for he would ground all his major fictional works in the immediacy of living history, giving his books a solidity and veracity for which he is now internationally respected.

During his three years as an undergraduate in history, Bhattacharya attended classes in four colleges of the University of London. One of them was the London School of Economics, where he read under the famous political philosopher and author, Harold Laski. This in itself, he says, was a "privilege" that made his going to London worthwhile. The association with Laski, in fact, would prove to be another formative experience in the making of a writer. Laski, at the London School of Economics from 1926 to the end of his life in 1950, attempted to apply the Marxist interpretation to what he saw as the present "crisis in democracy." A strong undercurrent of the early Marxist respect for liberal humanitarianism and the effects of economic pressures on history runs through all the Bhattacharya novels.

Bhattacharya acknowledges that throughout his years in London he was close to the Marxist group, for they were opposed to British imperialism in India. He became an active member of the Marxist-associated League Against Imperialism, among whose noted leaders was Jawaharlal Nehru. Although he was even then more creative writer than social activist, these early Marxist connections would follow him back to his homeland. In the early days of his return (1935) the C.I.D.,[2] he says, "trailed" him everywhere. Even earlier a high police officer in Calcutta had warned his father that his position as a judge was in jeopardy if his son continued his political activism in London.

The demands of study and political activity did not preclude creative writing. In his first year in London the young Bengali found time to write poems in his mother tongue and short prose sketches in English, some of which were sent back to be published in the Bengali magazine, *Vichitra*. One such was an article, "The English and the French." The English writing began to find its way into the highly respected *Manchester Guardian* and *The Spectator*. Bhattacharya considered better than acceptances and payments, the invitation from *Spectator* editor, Francis Yeats-Brown, to be his guest at lunch. This was the beginning of a long friendship with Yeats-Brown, who had just become a celebrity on the publication of his book of memoirs, *Lives of a Bengal Lancer*.

It was Yeats-Brown who urged Bhattacharya to concentrate on writing in English—advice that would later be affirmed by Tagore. The logic behind the editor's counsel was heady stuff for a neophyte writer—that English would assure him a world audience. "A world audience was nowhere in my calculations then!" Bhattacharya exclaimed, when telling me of the experience. But from this time on, he turned more and more to writing in English. Bengali went largely unused, since he found it "hardly possible to have two linguistic mediums for self-expression." Bengali, however, remains the language of thought and emotion. Even today, he says, he usually thinks in Bengali, then translates the thoughts into English. Authenticity and "flavor" are obtained by sometimes giving a Bengali phrase in literal translation. This is especially effective when simulating village dialogue. Reflecting on Bhattacharya's unique style, Robert Payne commented in *The Saturday Review*: " He writes in a language which is not English, yet all the words are English."

Bhattacharya's academic career continued at a leisurely pace— one suspects giving way frequently to the now consuming interest in writing. By this time he had become associated with several literary groups, foremost among which was the international literary club P.E.N., when the British novelist and dramatist, John Galsworthy, was president. Among his literary friends he remembers especially Lionel Britton, whose first novel, *Hunger and Love*, had just brought him fame.

At this period Bhattacharya resumed the translation of Tagore, begun when he was an undergraduate at Patna University. A number of his English versions were published in *The Spectator*, with Tagore's approval. When the poet came to London in 1930, Bhattacharya sought him out, for he now had greater maturity and was fortified by the assurance of Tagore's interest in his translations. The two agreed on a collection of the translations in book form. In that same year *The Golden Boat* was published, first in London and later in New York. More doors to literary circles flew open for Bhattacharya.

The award in 1931 of the Bachelor of Arts degree with Honors in History from the University of London was almost anticlimactic, for the limitations of the university sphere were restrictive compared with the expanding horizons of the writer's world.

Following three months vacation at home in India, Bhattacharya returned to the London scene to continue both study and writing. Soon thereafter he had his first meeting with Mohandas Gandhi, who was in the British capital for the famous Round Table Conference discussions on India's demand for independence. Bhattacharya tells of the time in history and in his life when he first met Gandhi face to face:

India's struggle for freedom had reached one of its peak points. I had been close to that struggle, though not an activist. In India I had attended many meetings in which Gandhi spoke. But this was my first encounter with the great man; it was only a little less overwhelming than the one with Tagore.

As will be pointed out elsewhere (especially in the discussions of *Shadow from Ladakh* and of *Gandhi the Writer*), the influence of Gandhi on Bhattacharya's thought and work would come to be more pervasive than that of any other personality, including even Tagore.

IV *European Encounters*

While continuing his doctoral studies at the University of London, in the two years between 1931 and 1933 Bhattacharya found—or took—time to travel extensively on the Continent. Though he had experienced much for a young man in his mid-twenties from remote Bihar, he little suspected that the time was not too far off when the products of his creative imagination would be translated into most of the major languages of Europe and that his characters—suffering, rejoicing, and growing through the situations in which he placed them—would be living realities to many of these people walking the worn cobblestones of Berlin, Warsaw, Paris, Vienna.

There was, however, some slight premonition of what was to come in an encounter Bhattacharya had during a boat trip on the Danube from Vienna to Budapest. On a visit to the Continent in 1932 Bhattacharya met Tagore again, this time in a lakeside mansion in Berlin. He notes that in those times of Nazi ascendancy the concept of Universal Man was in eclipse. Only a decade earlier four million copies of Tagore's books had been sold in German translation; now the poet's light was dimmed. Nevertheless, there were those who remembered and revered, and Asia's first Nobel Laureate was still a great figure among the culturally and spiritually aware.

When talking with a Hungarian woman at the dining table during the Danube trip, the conversation turned to Tagore. Bhattacharya revealed he knew the great man personally and was one of his authorized translators. "She was so impressed," he says, "that she pleaded with me to give her the honor of being the host of 'Tagore's translator' in Budapest!"

His Doctor of Philosophy degree in history obtained from the University of London in June 1934, Bhattacharya six months later returned to India. It would be close to two decades before he would again be in Europe. When he came back it would be as the established, often lionized, author, whose books had begun to appear in all the major languages of the Continent.

V *The Maturing Years*

Bhabani Bhattacharya had just turned twenty-eight when he went back to India in December 1934. With regard to years he had reached maturity. In terms of life-development he had only just completed the first of the four stages in the Hindu life pattern, the stage of *bramacharya*, an unmarried student.

One of the first concerns of Bhattacharya's parents, then, was to see their son married and entered upon the next stage of life. It was more than time that he marry, become a householder, raise a family, and find a dignified but lucrative position—in short, assume the traditional responsibilities of the *gàrhasthya*. In the Indian fashion, discreet inquiries were made to find a suitable wife, a young woman whose birth, education, and cultural interests would approximate those of the English-educated repatriate.

Bhattacharya has said that a "compulsive reason" for his accepting an "arranged" marriage was to meet the wishes of his mortally ill father. Although the marriage was to be settled according to ancient tradition, it would be modern to the extent that the young people would meet and accept or reject the proposed match. Despite six years of European education and travel and initial success as writer and Tagore translator, with his characteristic modesty, Bhabani did not regard himself an unqualified matrimonial asset. "At that time," he said, "I had nothing to show for myself—only a Ph.D."[3]

Bhattacharya and Salila Mukerji were introduced through friends not long after Bhabani had taken up bachelor residence in Calcutta. It was a meeting of "opposites" whose basic interests and life expectations were remarkably similar. The beautiful, vivacious, and outgoing young girl of seventeen had grown up in Nagpur in an atmosphere that combined English sophistication and ancient Indian culture. Her father, a prominent Bengali physician, was apparently a man with an unusually liberal and modern outlook. For one thing, he did not require as his daughter's husband a man well established in a productive career. The impecunious young man was recognized by his prospective father-in-law as having a wealth of promise.

Seven years after Dr. Mukerji's death, Bhattacharya affectionately recalled[4] the remarkable man who was Salila's father:

Though a physician of note, his heart was in literature, amazingly generous (he treated the poor free of charge and his charities were countless), he was one of the most remarkable—and lovable—men I have had the privilege to know. Much of my inspiration to be a writer (a hazardous decision anywhere, but more so in India) came from his warm support. Salila has inherited a great deal of his spirit—his human values and heart's warmth. It was for his sake that we could not leave Nagpur and settle elsewhere. Even today we continue to feel his benign presence.

The entire Mukerji family was sports-oriented, and Salila herself played badminton, tennis, and, in her childhood, even football. She shared the family enthusiasm for spectator sports. "She was brought up in an athletic world," Bhattacharya once exclaimed, "and I didn't even know how many members there are on a cricket team!"

Such differences in background and surface interests, however, were obviously superficial, for, from the moment they met the young people knew what they wanted. "When I met Salila, I didn't want my parents to look further," Bhattacharya says, adding with evident satisfaction, "She felt the same way. Four months later we were married."

Salila would bring into Bhabani's world new areas of interest, a different approach to life, a refreshingly unpedantic perspective. Above all, she would be his energetic collaborator. Open and warmly responsive to others, she helped bring the reclusive scholar out of his shell. Once when he referred to the years in Nagpur as affording him the peace necessary for his writing, Salila added: "But if we had lived in New Delhi you would have been more outgoing." "Outgoingness" would be one of her most affirmative contributions to the author and to the family.

Salila undoubtedly should be given large credit, also, for interpreting the woman's psyche for Bhattacharya, whose characterizations of women have stimulated increasing interest and scholarly study. In an interview with a news columnist in Australia,[5] Salila revealed the way in which she has opened a whole area of the inner human life to the writer:

Three of my husband's four novels [*Shadow from Ladakh* had not yet been published] have been centered in villages, and deal with the life of the inhabitants. While he is writing, we spend some of our time in villages, speaking to the people.

The Indian village women are not as emancipated as Australian women, and it would be very difficult for a man to suddenly begin talking to them.

I do not interview them, but just say "hello" or "may I have a glass of water." They realize I am from the city and are happy to talk to me. Later, my husband enters the hut and by this time the women are not afraid to talk to us both.

VI   *The Writer Is Born*

Soon after the marriage in June 1935, Bhattacharya began working on his first novel, *Music for Mohini*, which would become his
second major published work. When one knows the Bhattacharyas,
their characters and personality traits, the chronological logic of the
writing is apparent. In our talk together in their Honolulu apartment
in 1971, Salila Bhattacharya interrupted the beginning talk about
Music for Mohini to make the relevancy clear, saying to Bhabani:

Wasn't the predicament of Jayadev and Mohini really ours? You, the established scholar at 28; I, at 17 — — — Remember, you didn't want the traditional arranged marriage. You were against all the traditional Hindu proce-
dures. [Then, turning to me:] After we met through friends Bhabani wanted to
be married in seven days! That was an impossible thing to do for a Hindu
ceremony.

Bhattacharya accepted his wife's remarks and added:

Mohini and her background were just like my wife's. If I hadn't gone to
England I would have been somewhat like Jayadev. To a certain extent my
family was like Jayadev's. Though we lived in the city, we were orthodox
Hindu Brahmins. However, while my mother, like Jayadev's mother, did not
adjust her ideas, she did give complete freedom to others, and her love for her
daughter-in-law was without any reservations.

Replying to a scholar asking about possible similarities between
his wife and Suruchi in *Shadow from Ladakh*, Bhattacharya wrote
early in 1971:

I don't think Suruchi reflects my wife. It will be nearer the truth to say that
she and Mohini are of the same genre. Their backgrounds are alike, while I
had Jayadev's background—up to a point. My wife, brought up in "Westernized" lifeways, faced the compulsion of adjusting herself to a very different
psychological environment. And she did achieve the harmony needed—
enormous self-sacrifice was involved.

He also insists, however, that his characters in general are com-
posites. Not fully defined as his writing begins, they grow and
develop, changing from his original concept. Above all he refrains
from depicting his characters as stereotypes. "I don't have the
nineteenth-century mind that represents," he once told me. "Anyone

who has seen life with any sort of perceptivity knows there are no villains or heroes. Every villain has something of the hero in him, and every hero something of the villain, and you never know which is going to come out." Then he added, pensively, "One needs an elemental understanding of life before one dares to become a novelist."

Before leaving Salila to focus again on the career of her husband, it might be noted that Salila herself had done some writing as a young girl. Her short stories seemed "poor beside his," however, and she has attempted no creative writing since her marriage. Through the years she has been her husband's astute critic, typist, and (one suspects) frequent first editor. Surely, she has been his constant source of encouragement. Speaking of his initial writing on *Music for Mohini*, Bhattacharya in January 1971 confessed:

I thought I was no novelist and discarded (not destroyed) the manuscript. The years passed. Out of an emotional compulsion I wrote *So Many Hungers!* I would not have sent it to a publisher. My wife was watching the manuscript as it grew, and she forced me to mail it to Victor Gollancz in London. Prompt response came by way of a cable.

I returned to the discarded *Mohini*; rewrote some parts; added new material. This was my first book to be published in New York.

Turning to journalism for a livelihood, Bhattacharya in 1935 began contributing a biweekly feature to *The Statesman*, Calcutta, and a weekly feature, "This Week in Indian History," to *The Hindu*, Madras. In 1936 the couple visited Rabindranath Tagore at Santiniketan. A photo of Tagore and Bhattacharya, taken by Salila, at this time, shows an obviously awed and shy young man in Western dress, knees together, hands clutching his arms, seated beside the impressive figure of his "Gurudev" in flowing robe, the strong yet sensitive features almost completely lost in long white locks and beard.

It was then that Tagore urged him to remain at the ashram-school as teacher and writer. "He even assigned me to a house renowned as 'the tree-house,'" Bhattacharya recalled. "Architecturally unique, the house was built around a tree whose trunk went up through the roof of the living room. Of his own design, the poet himself had lived there. To have that house meant honor."

Though the invitation was flattering and tempting, Bhattacharya declined. He felt that if he was to realize his own identity as an author

he would have to work at a greater distance from Tagore's overwhelming personality. He had no wish to be a mere echo of the
great poet.

In 1937, after the death of Bhabani's father, the young couple
moved to Nagpur, and it was there that son Arjun was born in
November, the birth month of his father.

The next four years passed with no notable change in pace, but,
looking back, they may be viewed as part of the maturing process.
Though the mind of the historian and the sensitivities of the creative
artist would have been alert to the tragic turmoil that was building
up to cataclysmic proportions in Europe, the comparative calm and
cyclic passage of time in Nagpur screened the young family from
direct involvement. It would not be until the great Bengal famine of
1943, coinciding as it did with the impingement of the European War
on the sub-continent, that the novelist would be born with the publication of *So Many Hungers!* in 1947.

Social forces and inequities would always be the source of Bhattacharya's inspiration and his compulsion to write. "My chief purpose
is to deal with the problems of social change," he has said. "I see
fiction as a means to this end."

Bhattacharya has revealed that although he and his family were
not directly affected by the carnage accompanying the partition of
India and Pakistan in 1947 (see Chapter 1), the tragic events of that
year forced him into publication:

> During Partition we were all in Nagpur, so we didn't have any direct ex-
> perience of the trauma. One point may interest you. The trauma was disastrous
> for Indian economy. The stocks in which my inheritance from my father . . .
> had been invested crashed and became virtually scraps of paper. Hence, I had
> to take my literary *profession* very much more seriously! I was going slow over
> *Hungers*. I rushed to complete the manuscript. Luckily, good royalties came
> from many countries. An unexpected windfall from Sweden where it sold
> 30,000 copies.[6]

VII *The International Man*

From this point on the writer became increasingly involved in
national and international life—as a press attaché at the Embassy of
India in Washington; as a cultural ambassador to Russia, West
Germany, England, New Zealand, Australia; as a participant in
international literary seminars held at Harvard, in Tokyo, and else-

where; as a research scholar at the East-West Center in Honolulu and visiting professor at the University of Hawaii; and as an honored guest at the Universities of Washington (Seattle) and British Columbia (Vancouver).

But the soul of the creative writer still dominated the outwardly active life, leading Bhattacharya to a high point of official national recognition in his own country when in 1968 he received from the President of India the Sahitya Akademi Award, India's highest literary honor. Though stimulated by the publication of *Shadow from Ladakh*, his fifth novel, the award statement made clear the honor was based on a lifetime of literary achievement. The citation noted him as a "distinguished author and novelist . . . a writer of considerable sensitivity and charm . . . [who] has depicted a cross-section of contemporary India during a period of transition and rapid development, and has reflected the intricate pattern of present-day life with a remarkable understanding and clarity."

There have been other impressive recognitions of the solidly established and widely respected author—such as the fairly recent scholarly research and writing on Bhattacharya by critics (exploring his social themes, his skill in portraying women characters in English, etc.) and by doctoral candidates; the 1973 Walker-Ames lectureship at the University of Washington, Seattle, extended to Bhattacharya as one of "the most distinguished minds available"; and, finally, as an author whose published works, manuscripts, and biographical materials are now assembled in the Bhabani Bhattacharya Collection in the Special Collections repository of the Boston University libraries.

Immersion in the Hawaii scene (which Bhabani and Salila came to love) and close acquaintance with American youth promise to reactivate the creative process, from which a sixth novel is expected to emerge. It is inevitable that new writing will either arise from or in some way utilize the American scene, for Bhattacharya has revealed he and his wife have "virtually said goodbye" to Nagpur.[7] The invitation to the East-West Center came on the heels of the Ford Foundation's travel award and the stay in the United States has been indefinitely extended.

Bhattacharya has spoken often of the appeal of the East-West Center at the University of Hawaii and of the impact on his life and thought made during his year there as a member of its Senior Specialist Program in the Institute of Advanced Projects. The

Center, which was established by the United States Congress as a meeting ground for cultural and technical interchange between scholars and specialists from Asia and the West, fortified the author's life-long dedication to intercultural and interpersonal cooperation and accommodation. His prospectus for independent research and writing while at the Center, entitled "South and Southeast Asia: Some Strategies of Solidarity," opens with a statement of purpose consonant with his lifetime of writing:

> This study, in its conceptual framework, is meant to be multi-disciplinary. It will cover intercultural history (including religion), education, economics, and other areas of the social sciences. While the analysis will be mainly concerned with Southeast Asian development, it will include an examination of South Asia's potential capacity to make a contribution in this regard by way of transfer of knowledge, experience, and various techniques.

After citing problems in development, economic growth, and regional factionalism, he concludes:

> In my research plan I seek practical answers to these intricate problems, *so that multiform cooperation may not appear as a mere wish-thought* and an empty phrase. The wide-ranging symbols and instruments of solidarity, as I see them, are interlocked in Southeast Asia development. [Italics are mine.]

VIII *"A Dream in Hawaii"*

In a letter written (December 18, 1973) some time after the East-West Center year, Bhattacharya noted the significance of the experience in terms of his life's thought and creative work. He also gave his most explicit (if a "dream" may be called "explicit"!) expression to date of the creative impetus it had provided:

> I should add a few words in regard to the East-West Center's impact on me. Interculturation, in a broad sense of the term, is one of the key elements in two of my novels [*Music for Mohini* and *Shadow from Ladakh*]. . . . Hence, when I saw another dimension of the same idea institutionalized at the East-West Center, I felt pleased.
>
> The East-West Center with its unique human content along with its concrete realizing of "interculturation" in terms of lifeways has illustrated for me over again what Tagore's Visva-Bharati (World University) envisioned several decades ago. And I value this experience very deeply, indeed. Perhaps I may be able to dramatize some of this stuff of experience in a novel I have in

view, tentatively titled *A Dream in Hawaii*. That, of course, will be just one of the dimensions of the story, which is itself a dream so far.

It has been an exciting experience for me to observe how the novelist's mind works on an incident or series of real-life events to create his world of fiction. While still at the University of Hawaii, Bhattacharya was intrigued and excited by the overwhelming, almost pathetic, response of the students to lectures and meditation sessions being held by visiting "*swamis*" and "*gurus*" from India. He told of attending a mass conclave at the East-West Center's 2,000 seat theater when such a lecture was given. "The place was packed with young people," he said, "sitting in the aisles, standing at the rear. Their faces displayed their hunger for spiritual nourishment." I had little doubt but that this would form the basic stuff for his next work. Indeed, as this study goes to press, it is evident that the Hawaii "Dream" has come to focus on this recent phenomenon in American student life.

On October 15, 1974, Bhattacharya wrote that his first "American novel" was being sent in increments to Millen Brand, his long-time editor at Crown Publishers, and that Brand's response has been enthusiastic. He quoted Brand as commenting: "You're making your novel convincing in the main configuration." Concerning the book itself, Bhattacharya wrote on that date:

A Dream in Hawaii ... is a total departure for me, being an American novel—American even in Hawaii. The characters are both Americans and Asians; the setting is Today. The core concern of the story is the current disenchantment in the Great Society and the intense, fretful strivings to find an answer to one's life, to find the path of one's self-fulfillment. ... The American content of the novel is a challenge which I have immensely enjoyed.

CHAPTER 3

So Many Hungers!

I *Situation and Setting*

IN this his first published novel Bhattacharya is inspired by a world event that is both peripheral to the personal human involvement and is the cause of crisis situations in the lives of individuals who are central to the story. In *So Many Hungers!* the macrocosmic world is reflected and intensified in the microcosm of Bengali life.

The action opens in the Calcutta home of Rahoul, who is anxiously awaiting the birth of his first child. His attention, however, is divided between listening for an infant's cry and concentrating on radio news of the outbreak of war in Europe.

The meaning of this far-off conflict for the Basu family is made apparent in swift-moving summary and dialogue. For Rahoul's mother it means hasty accumulation of food and clothing against inevitable shortages. For younger brother Kunal it is enlistment in the cavalry of His Majesty's armed forces. For the father it offers a golden opportunity for financial speculation. Before long Samarendra, the father, is immersed in stock manipulations and black market operations.

While Rahoul ponders his reaction to world events, his daughter, Khuku, is born. Typically, this milestone in his personal life is equated with one in the international sphere:

The scream! The thin, helpless, persistent scream of a new-born one! Rahoul stood rooted. The elation that made his heart swell! Two exciting things had happened to him this autumn day. The Prime Minister of Britain had declared war on the Swastika. Monju had given birth to a baby girl. Either event was a profound experience that made his emotions vibrate, as though he had achieved some personal fulfillment.

In the blood-bath of war much else would be drowned besides the Swastika. A million youths would not die in vain. (17)[1]

Events of world significance are noted in passing, naturally, as they have impact on the lives of the characters. The landing of the Allies at Dunkirk in 1940, for instance, is mentioned only as it has meaning in connection with Samarendra's shady speculations. After having realized unbelievable profits, the market crash of that year stuns him. It recovers quickly, however, and he manages to liquidate his holdings just before the fall of Singapore (1942) and a final crash. His dream of an English title, "bought" by contributions to Britain's War Fund, seem possible of fulfillment, after all. He turns next to trying to corner Bengal's rice market.

II *Nationalism*

While his father is using the war for his own financial and social advancement, Rahoul finds himself increasingly involved in India's independence movement. He is, in fact, experiencing a rebirth of old allegiances initially formed during his student years at Cambridge. When first back from his years abroad, the trauma of Europe had seemed more real to him than that at home. Now he is torn by a variety of conflicting loyalties: home and family, scientific research that has power potential for peace or war, participation in what he sees as civilization's greatest "war of liberation," or the liberation of his homeland for which many patriots were now imprisoned. He needs the inner vision that only his grandfather, Dadu, can help him attain.

Rahoul's visit with his grandfather in the village of Baruni establishes the tenuous link that joins the narrative line between the Calcutta and Baruni characters. For here Rahoul meets and is moved by the warmheartedness and simple goodness of that "other family" with whom Dadu lives a simple village life.

To Rahoul's question as to what hope the common people of India can have, his grandfather answers:

" . . . The national movement gives top priority to village reconstruction work, that you know. This is the very basis of our life to come. The Government do not like it, of course. They and the landlords have grown to fear the peasant masses. Once, not many years ago, odd to think, they posed as champions of the voiceless people against the intellectual classes, the sedition-mongers who talk of freedom for all. But the times have changed, the mask has blown off, the real face lies revealed. . . . Mass literacy is a danger for the rulers. It would, they know, make the trampled ones conscious of their birth-right—the right to live as human beings." (24)

Rahoul returns to Calcutta imbued with the Nationalist spirit. He continues with his research as usual, however, and bides his time.

Eventually, Rahoul learns that Prokash, his laboratory assistant, is active in underground Nationalist activity. Now the two work together as political activists as well as research scientists.

With the Japanese battle fleet in the Bay of Bengal, British authorities round up all moored boats to prevent their being taken and used by the enemy. Though the fishermen of Baruni are paid in gold for their scuttled boats, what is that worth when a family's livelihood has been stripped away? They rise up against their rulers:

"We curse you. We curse your dear ones. We curse your butcher masters. May you, too, burn like that; *nah*, may you, too, and your masters stand by and see your lives burn like that. We curse you all."

As the blaze died down and the boat-wreckers moved off in their motor-launch, the fisher-folk stepped to the burnt wreckage, and each man picked up a handful of hot cinders and tied it to the corner of his *dhoti*. Then down the midnight path they walked back in utter silence, their heads bent, their bodies and souls burnt and destroyed. (58)

After Burma falls (1941), the Government begins a scorched earth movement throughout the villages to deter enemy forces from advancing into India. The peasants will be compensated, they are assured. But higher returns may be reaped from city predators who offer local merchants tempting sums for their rice. Despite the warnings of Rahoul's grandfather, the peasants and merchants of Baruni, one by one, yield to prices higher than they had ever dreamed of. Their hunger for wealth is sated by the life hunger of the masses.

III   *Disorder, Revolt, Famine*

With the Japanese at the gates of Bengal and the Nationalist movement gaining impetus, the British in India are threatened on two fronts—by alien forces impinging along the Burma Road and by rebellious "colonials."

Following the arrests of Nehru, Gandhi, and other leaders, a spontaneous peoples' revolt breaks out and is violently suppressed. Rahoul is briefly imprisoned. There is violence, also, in the village,

and Dadu, his son-in-law, and grandson are jailed. Bereft of the
old man's steadying influence, the village succumbs increasingly
to the black market enticements:

> "Brother, this is your true chance. Sell all you can. Eight *rupees* for a *maund*
> of rice. . . . Ever heard of such a price in a hundred and one years and in all
> the days of your fourteen generations? It is as though your paddy is dyed
> with water-of-gold!" (80)

Between such predators and oppressive government taxes, the
village of Baruni—like thousands of villages the length and breadth
of India—is left drained.

In contrast to mounting tragedy at home, Kunal, Rahoul's
younger brother, writes almost joyously from the war front. He
recounts the victories of the Indian army in the Libyan desert,
finding in them a new affirmation of race pride:

> "Our soldiers from India have won a great victory, I am proud to say,"
> he wrote. "I don't mean their victory over the enemy, I mean their victory,
> as it were, over themselves. You see, *dada*, they have killed their old foe—the
> sense of race inferiority. . . . The soldiers from India have fought and defeated
> white troops in pitched battles even against very heavy odds. The white man's
> bubble has exploded in the African air . . . the myth that has been the spine
> of empire lies in pieces on the desert sands." (107)

Famine sweeps the land. Rahoul hears of it at "the pleasant
lakeside" where he lives:

> The empty stomach was due to no blight of Nature, no failure of crops
> Rahoul knew. It was man-made scarcity . . . with rationing at the right level
> there could be food for all. But there was no rationing. . . . Inflated currency
> added the finishing touch. (108)

There is no revolt against famine such as there had been against
colonialism. The peasants—chief sufferers—see starvation as their
personal *karma*:

> They would not rise in revolt that their stomachs could be soothed—a selfish
> personal end! They would fight and die over a moral issue. But hunger was
> their fate, an expiation of the sins of past lives. The peasants' hands were
> manacled with their antique moral tradition. (111)

The peasants now trade any possessions they may have for small quantities of rice, or even sell their cattle (most valued possessions) in order to buy rice at five times the price for which they had sold it a few months earlier. And dealers bide their time for more cattle and even for the land itself.

Having seen their rice and cattle sold to the cities, the village folk believe food will be found there. They begin the exodus cityward.

Dadu's granddaughter, Kajoli, however, clings to the land. Eventually she is left with no more than the family cow, too starved to give milk, too loved to be sold, and too revered to be eaten. Only when their cattle are at death's door do the peasants consider selling them to dealers who furnish the army with meat. And then, those that do are horrified at the thought that there are men who are willing to eat the sacred flesh.

Bhattacharya traces the eventual exodus of Kajoli, her mother and young brother from Baruni, ironically, just as the fields are expected to produce a bumper crop of rice.

The journey toward the "Utopia" of Calcutta is marked by harrowing days of starvation, the rape of Kajoli, and the ultimate degradation of life on the city streets. Instead of the Promised Land, the misery they have known is compounded a thousand times over in the lives of the city's poor among the refugees who have left their land only to die in alien streets. Bhattacharya's description of human starvation is grim with authenticity:

Strange how much a human body could go through before life left it at last. The first few days man suffered most. He was mad with hunger. Then he grew listless. He laid himself down. His mouth was too tired for food, and he only wanted to be left alone. His eyes died. He wasted to a skeleton, using up whatever shreds of flesh he had anywhere on his body. (160)

IV Conclusion

The author deals in irony after irony as he brings his bitter account to a conclusion. While Rahoul and his once impractical wife, Monju, direct and work in the food kitchen to which their village cousins resort daily for their mid-day meal of rice gruel, they never meet. The beautiful Kajoli determines to sell herself into prostitution just as her mother sets out to drown herself in the sacred Ganges in order to relieve Kajoli of the burden of her existence.

In a series of reversals, Kajoli is rescued from her shame and the mother from drowning. Or *is* the mother saved? The book ends with much left to the reader's imagination.

The story comes full circle in the concluding chapter, returning to Rahoul's father, the enterprising financier. Samarendra becomes a Companion of the Indian Empire—C.I.E.—as he had dreamed of becoming at the outset of the action. In a final irony, however, this is as dust in his nostrils when he learns simultaneously that Kunal, his light-hearted younger son, is missing in action, in all probability dead, and that Rahoul has been arrested for his outspoken opposition to India's participation in a "colonialist war."

The story closes as Rahoul enters prison, exultant rather than disheartened:

> He was alone and in enemy hands. Yet he was far from alone. He was a ripple in the risen tide of millions for whom prisons enough could never be devised, nor shackles forged. And strong exultation burned in his eyes and a strange intense look of conquest kindled in his face. (215)

V *Factual Backgrounds*

In observations on the art of literary criticism ("Hollow Arbiters of the Writer's Destiny") Bhattacharya tells something concerning the launching of this, his first published novel. The manuscript, sent simultaneously to a Bombay and to a London publisher, was accepted immediately by the Bombay firm and published within a matter of months. Bhattacharya remembers his mixed emotions on reading first reviews, so venemous they convinced him he "was not destined to be a creative writer" (see Chapter 8).

Soon after, however, the book was also issued in London, followed by many favorable notices. Final success was assured at home when the Governor of Uttar Pradesh mentioned the novel favorably during a news interview. The resultant publicity turned the tide of opinion.

The book has borne up well through the years, although it can be seen in retrospect as distinctly the maiden effort of a new and promising novelist. Bhattacharya, himself, has called this first book "very unstructured." Later books would show more mastery of form, and one almost ten years later—*He Who Rides a Tiger*—would use almost the identical substance with more maturity and assurance.

It is not unusual for an author to write himself into one of the major characters of his fictional work, especially his first. On first reading *So Many Hungers!* I was struck by Rahoul's resemblance to Bhattacharya and asked the author whether this character was, indeed, himself. His reply was, "I may have projected myself into many of my characters, but never consciously so." Whether consciously or not, the Rahoul of *So Many Hungers!* would appear to be the Bhabani Bhattacharya of real life. Not only are the values of Rahoul apparently those of Bhattacharya, but one who knows the author is struck by similar physical characteristics. Of Rahoul, Bhattacharya writes: "His eyes behind the thick-rimmed glasses were keen and alight." So might the author see his own eyes reflected in his morning mirror. Rahoul, like his creator, laughs in a "silent inward way." Rahoul, too, is slight and not too tall (specifically, two inches shorter than his younger brother, Kumal). And he is the visionary, the dreamer, unlike Kumal whose "practical mind" Rahoul reluctantly admires as being "untroubled by theories of right and wrong."

Even though the author and his central urban character may seem soul brothers, nevertheless it is in his depiction of peasant character and peasant life that the author excels. Perhaps in Rahoul and his milieu the author is too close to himself to write with perspective and ease. Self-revelation is never a wholly easy process. For whatever reason, it is only after Bhattacharya becomes immersed in the peasant scene that his writing comes fully to life.

Although the opening chapters give a sense of movement and reveal characters and their relationships through action and dialogue, rather than by exposition, construction tends to be fragmentary and abrupt. Too many sentences without verbs, and a succession of disjointed phrases, give the reader a feeling of studied straining for effect.

This modern—almost impressionistic—manner is sometimes oddly mixed with a certain Victorian sentimentality. On the first page, for instance, the reader moves from the opening, disjointed phrases reflective of Rahoul's impression of radio news reports to a look into the mind of his mother as she thinks about him. The first so modern; the second so outdated. Or is it an odd mixture? Is the author not reflecting in his shift in style the different modes of thought in two generations—son and mother?

The deliberately fragmentary style (the "staccatto style of Steinbeck," Bhattacharya once called it) lends itself well to depiction
of frenetic financial dealings at the Calcutta Stock Exchange in
the opening days of the war:

> Pulses pounding. The blood beating in the ears. The crowd with cash in
> the banks, cash to play with. Buy munitions of war—things that make guns,
> shells. Buy Steels. War eats steel. . . .
> SELL! Cash in your profits. This isn't like the last War. Going to be short.
> Only a blitz. Peace in a year. . . .
> BUY! Cotton for the Army. Troops to be sheathed in uniform. . . . Uni-
> forms wasted on dead bodies. Boots. Woollens. . . . (15–16)

However, it is only as the author becomes totally absorbed by
his subject matter and gets deeper into the experience of hardship
and starvation that his style ceases to be self-conscious and becomes
a natural vehicle for his subject. It is in the village and among the
peasants that the tragedy of famine is most fully experienced, and
it is in these portions of the novel that expression and content reach
their finest fusion.

VI *The Writer's Role*

Bhattacharya has said that *So Many Hungers!* was written from
a compulsion to record for the widest possible reading public the
intense suffering of the people of India during the famine of 1943.
His fictional representation was based on fact—personal observation or news accounts of actual incidents. As he himself has pointed
out, however, hunger is used metaphorically as well as specifically
and realistically. The word arises out of the many varieties of
hungers, he has said.[2] There is not only the hunger for food, but
for freedom, money, sex (as seen in "the sex mania of the new
capitalists"). There is also Rahoul's hunger for self-fulfillment—as
an intellectual, as a scientist, as a freedom fighter, as a worker for
social reform. In Rahoul these several hungers sometimes combine
and strengthen one another as they work in accord; at other times
they conflict and tear him apart, as when his increasing involvement
in the freedom movement disrupts his scientific research.

I recall Bhattacharya's reading to a university seminar group
the following scene of the artist and the dead mother and discussing

with them the differing roles of the creative artist and the social worker. The incident is seen—significantly—through the eyes of Rahoul (Bhattacharya).

A knot of people had formed at the far end of the [railway] platform. Sharp words, sharp gestures of anger. A row? Rahoul walked on to the crowd.

The centre of the commotion was a man who sat on a large packing-case, a pencil in his hand, stooping over a writing-pad. Some yards away on the platform, half concealed by another packing-case, a destitute woman lay on her side, her legs drawn up, eyes closed, a baby at her breast. The woman lay still, but the baby moved its lips faintly as it suckled.

The mother was dead.

A ticket-collector had seen, as he strolled by, the man on the packing-case and the famished woman, motionless on the ground. He had drawn close, curious, peering down at the paper tablet. An artist making a pencil sketch of the woeful little group. Destitutes were not allowed on platforms . . . she would have to be turned out, miserable one. The unhappy ticket-collector cleared his throat and gave the order. No response. . . . The collector stepped close and cried out in horror. She was dead!

"She is dead," the railwayman said to the artist, his voice toneless.

"Hoon," said the other, deep in his work.

"You knew?" Eyes amazed, brows drawn.

Yes, he knew. He knew that the child was suckling the breast of its dead mother.

"This is very odd. You didn't consider it your duty to report to us? The mother dead, the child alive, suckling - - - "

The artist lifted his eyes for a quick instant. "Let me work in peace." And he drew the lines. . . .

"If you had any sense of decency, any human feeling, you would have reported. . . ." The railwayman had a clouded, scornful face. . . .

"Do not distract me, I beg of you," pleaded the other, and a swift bitterness hit his tone. "What am I doing but trying to make a report? Not to the railway people. I have to report to India."

The collector lost his temper then. "You brute!" People came rushing to the scene, drawn by the magnetism of a row, and they glared at the man, while the indignant collector cited his facts. . . .

They stood by, the bunch of people, jeering at the artist, but he spoke no word in self-defense; he seemed withdrawn from his accusers, unaware of their presence. His face grew tense. He was lost altogether in his work, now looking at the destitute group, now drawing a line, a curve.

A stout, well-fed man advanced to the artist. He snatched the pencil from the artist's hand and flung it far on the rail-track. When he had returned to the assault, the artist, wakened from his absorption, concealed the pad in his tunic. "What madness!" he cried. He looked about, at this face, at that face, in utter bewilderment.

The crowd went crazy. It rushed upon him beating him with cruel fists, snatching at the pad, while the victim, felled to the ground, desperately shielded his possession with his body.

The unequal struggle lasted a minute or two, and the sketch was captured and torn to pieces and the block of paper flung away.

Then the artist sat up, bruised, panting hard. . . . "Fools!" he cried, and the voice was shrill between sharp-drawn breaths. "Fools! You think you have destroyed my fancy. I shall yet make my report. India will see that dead mother nursing her child. . . ."

Rahoul slipped down to the rail-track, collected pencil and pad, handed them to their owner.

"Good writing-paper is scarce these days," he said, "unless you pay black-market rates."

The artist gazed at him in a distraught way.

"Bad luck," Rahoul went on. "Those fellows didn't know what they were doing. They hit you? No, they hit the mother lying dead. You have the picture within you. Let India see the picture. . . ."

Neither spoke for a time. The artist seemed to be struggling with some inward pain. His face brooded. When he spoke, his voice was heavy with emotion.

"What will happen to the child? I have neglected my duty, it is true. So much time thrown away. The child needs immediate care.". . .

Rahoul stared at him. The artist had lost his detachment, and, with detachment, vision. He seethed with human feeling.

Rahoul heaved an unhappy sigh. It seemed to him as though the dead mother on the platform nursing her tiny one now died for the second time. (161–164)

Here, it seems to me, Bhattacharya was not only reporting a moment of human suffering that he himself had seen (as he told that group of students) but was summing up his philosophy as a writer. His role in life is to be sensitive to (but not sentimental about) the human condition and get it into words that will capture it for the widest possible reading public and for posterity. His role is not the noble, but comparatively limited one, of the social worker, ministering to a specific human need. If the artist allows himself to be coerced into that role, he is subverting his creative function.

In fact, the scene just quoted presents the fictionalized quintessence of a major turn taken by Bhattacharya in his own life. As an impressionable young man he first met Gandhi in London, soon after the Great Salt March (see Chapter 9, "Biographer"). Through the dramatic action of several hundred of India's ordinary people a great nation had been moved to reverse an oppressive and unjust governmental policy. Should not Bhattacharya, like the Mahatma, become an activist in the Freedom Movement? But Tagore, whom he met somewhat later, convinced him that his contribution might better be made through his writing.

It is in scenes such as this that Bhattacharya achieves his finest writing. Poverty, starvation, homelessness, all are depicted as they are experienced by individuals who have aspired to more and who, in general, have deserved more.

All Bhattacharya characters—no matter how minor—are flesh-and-blood human beings. Though some (such as the merchant, Girish, and Rahoul's father, Samarendra) have certain stereotyped characteristics, they rise above such limitations and take on fully individual roles. Bhattacharya also avoids attributing all good or all bad to any one socioeconomic group. Although Kajoli and her mother resist the efforts made to draw Kajoli into prostitution, there are village women who succumb. Even Kajoli, herself, in final desperation, agrees to sell herself, being saved only by a rather too fortuitious turn of events. And Samarendra's greedy selfishness is not an urban or a class attribute, for the village storekeeper has the same failings.

VII *Time and Setting*

In *So Many Hungers!* the passage of time is realized by the reader through experiencing natural life events with the characters and through observing characters develop and change.

The novel begins with the beginning of life for Rahoul's daughter, Khuku. Toward the end of the action she is a small child of four playing "horsie" with her grandfather. Her mother, Monju, develops in stature from the spoiled child-wife who protests when Rahoul leaves her to visit the village, to the woman who, four years later, has come to share her husband's social concern and his work in behalf of the poor and the starving.

As in all his books, Bhattacharya gives a good sense of the Indian setting. Here, too, he attempts to be unobtrusive and nondidactic. Perhaps he assumes too much, however, for the reader completely unfamiliar with the background. The mere mechanics of a glossary might be helpful. Although Indian terms are often explained by their context, for the non-Indian reader too many are left without benefit of explanation. The reader would, for instance, get a much better appreciation of the levels of poverty with which *Hungers* is concerned if American or English equivalents were given for *rupee, anna, pice.*

But constant insights are given into customs and ways of life. There is the scene in which Rahoul observes Monju suffering in childbirth (and, here, how much more meaningful the passage would be if Yama were identified as the God of Death):

He saw the pupils of her eyes dilate, stained with deepening dread, as though Yama had tramped out of the night and stood at her bedside, in his hand the soul-holding tube into which he slipped life-sparks as he collected them, bits of phosphorescence. (7–8)

And the traditional welcome into a village home:

Kajoli was undoing his shoe-lace! Flurried, Rahoul pulled off his shoes— leathern shoes, he knew, were not to be worn beyond the doorstep. But the girl, Kajoli, was stooping still, . . . and out of the vessel she poured cool water on Rahoul's feet to wash off road dust. (25)

We become acquainted with the peasant love for cattle—the cow as much a part of the family as any human member. Even in times of most dire need, Mangala, the cow, should be provided for, not sold:

A great Army, it was said, was covering all Bengal, *paltan* of all races, many eaters of beef. Cattle drained swiftly out of villages. But the traders wondered sometimes at the selfishness deep in the peasant's marrowbones: to hold on to useless cattle while your children famished! (122)

Finally, Bhattacharya manages a poetic simulation of peasant speech through using a somewhat archaic English. This dialogue seems to advance the reality of the portions of the novel portraying village customs and to give an authenticity that is sometimes lacking in the scenes depicting life among the high-born city folk.

VIII   *Action Full Circle*

As the novel begins with a quick, staccato pace, so it also ends. In the few final pages Kunal is reported missing in battle, Rahoul is taken to prison, Samarendra receives his coveted C.I.E. and is advised that his eagerly-awaited rice deal is about to go through, Kajoli accepts and rejects prostitution in favor of selling newspapers on the street corner (a rather unworthy *deus ex machina?*), and Kajoli's mother is seen by Rahoul without recognition as she draws back from jumping from the Ganges bridge along which he passes on his way to prison, her fate unresolved for us as for him. One has the uncomfortable feeling of too many threads too hastily and too neatly tied up; too many ironies coalesced. The denouement would have been more effective, perhaps, if it were less tidy—more Chekovian in human imprecision.

But one should not worry over technicalities. From the English original (published in 1947 by Victor Gollancz, London) *So Many Hungers!* has found its way into ten or more languages of Europe and back into dialects of the author's own country. A book club selection in Great Britain, a best seller in various languages (including Chinese and Swedish), this first novel has spoken to hundreds of thousands of readers around the world.

CHAPTER 4

Music for Mohini

I *Mohini, the Girl*

MUSIC for Mohini is undoubtedly Bhattacharya's most light-hearted novel. Although social concern is present in the depiction of misunderstanding and animosities between village and city and between Old and New India, one has the feeling that Mohini, her dreams and her disappointments, her romances and her sometimes serious endeavors, take over despite her creator. To be sure, the author intends that the social conflicts should be dramatized and personalized in the life experience of the mercurial young heroine. But her personality so dominates that the reader may not become consciously concerned with the novel's social purposes. For here is a story drenched in the light and color of "Golden Bengal" and brightened by the laughter and song of Mohini, her brother, and her young friends.

Within the first two or three pages the reader is given a clear insight into Mohini's character. She revels in the warmth and the color of life. She cannot "bear images of decay." She loves to laugh. She is keenly aware, always seeing everything. She is devoted to her scholarly father, is respectful of her grandmother ("Old Mother"), and is the teasing companion of her younger brother. She is incurably romantic, convinced that every young man she knows is secretly in love with her.

Although not yet eighteen, Mohini has achieved some independent status in life as a recording artist and a radio singer. Father considers Mohini still a child, but to Old Mother she has been a woman for four years, and it is a matter of real concern that no overtures toward marriage have yet been made. She protests to Mohini's father: "Not even a horoscope! The sun and the moon will surely stand witness that I have poured a hundred cries in

your ear, childling: 'The daughter of the house will be the laugh
of the town unless you find her a groom.'" (18)[1] These old forms
are mere superstitions to the son, however: "'Luck signs. Horoscopes. What rubbish!' His voice was mocking. 'There's to be a
cultural synthesis of a horoscope and a microscope!'" (60)

Mohini is shaped by her environment. The rich variety of Calcutta she at once accepts and delights in. She has had no experience
beyond it. The noise and clamor and color of the streets and shops
are accepted parts of her life. Scholars and students come and go
from Father's study. Every day brings association with young
friends, priests, artisans, vendors, shopkeepers, household servants.
Although Old Mother holds the family to the forms of Brahmin
life and worship, in the face of city pressures even she has made
accommodation.

This first third of the book, devoted to the city scene, is crowded
with an almost bewildering gallery of characters, quickly shifting
situations and scenes, and an interplay of the opposing forces of
ancient custom and insistent change.

There is the brassy, ubiquitous Bindu, who, thwarted by caste
restrictions, turns to an abortive romance with the Snake Charmer
and to petty machinations against Mohini. There is the Cook-
woman, Bindu's mother, insistent of her rights, and judgmental
equally of those above and below her. There is the Snake Charmer,
who can charm maiden as well as serpent, and whose ancient stories
of snakes and cobra kings delight the young Heeralal.

II   *Marriage*

Under the pressure of Old Mother's insistence and Mohini's
obvious readiness for marriage, Father finally begins to take appro-
priate steps. He studies and clips the marriage ads in the daily
paper, then enters one in her behalf:

> Wanted a suitable match for a handsome,
> educated maid of charming disposition.
> Highly gifted radio singer. (39)

The reader is given an intimate insight into the humor and
the pathos of a marriage market governed by such advertisements
and by marriage bureaus. Mohini is caught in the anomaly of

being too Westernized for some prospects and too old fashioned for others. She seems precisely at the crossroads between the ways of Old Mother and those of independent India and emancipated womanhood.

Eventually, the way leads to Roop-lekha, wife of a Calcutta physician and sister of Jayadev, Master of Behula, noted Vedic scholar, whose published essays Father knows and whose published photo Mohini has secretly admired. The match seems perfect to Old Mother and to Mohini, herself. Only Father hesitates. How can his city-bred, freedom-loving daughter be happy "in a village among old-world folk"? Wonder of wonders, however, even the horoscopes of the young couple auspiciously conjoin.

So the marriage is agreed upon and the traditional observances precede the ceremony. After the final vows have been taken under the sheltering bridal shawl, husband and wife see each other face to face for the first time:

> Jayadev gazed, while Mohini's head dropped, her face flushed. . . . His looks meant little. She prayed only for his approval, his contentment.
> A hundred thousand Hindu maids each bridal day of the year give their hearts to their unknown husbands, asking nothing in return but approval. (74)

So Mohini leaves this home where love and security, wit and wisdom, laughter and music, old ways and new, have surrounded her throughout her life. She will recall Old Mother's final words again and again during the years ahead: "'Honor your mother-in-law as though she were your mother, and abide by her will. Answer her hot words with absolute silence. Sweeten your speech when you talk to your neighbors. Words dipped in honey cost nothing. Bend yourself to the customs and traditions of the village. . . .'" (78)

III *Journey into the Past*

There follows the overnight train trip, where the couple travel in separate compartments for men and women. The tortuous trip by bullock cart. The final, slow progress in palanquins borne on sweating human shoulders.

Mohini's journey into her unknown life may be seen as symbolic; her future, a probing into India's ancient village-centered past, which is at once past, present, and future of a culture. The "fire-breathing" train, symbol of modern technology, is first link to the countryside. The bullock cart, slow and ponderous as it may be, yet travels roadways that link rural life with urban. But beyond them are the still undisturbed meadows, through which wheels have yet to find their way, penetrated only by narrow foot trails to India's yesterdays.

And Jayadev the scholar dreams of Mohini herself as a mystic link between past and future. Will she not become a modern-day Maitreyi, that paragon of Vedic womanhood, wise and strong, equal participant in the struggle to make life meaningful and free?

His heart warmed to Mohini. . . . Out of the mist of the past the Vedic woman took form, the woman who had been the spiritual font of the greatest thinker of his age. It came on him, then, that this fusion of personalities was symbolic of the deeper fusion of which he dreamed, a profound union of today with yesterday. (92)

IV   *The Village*

So Mohini enters her new life with a weight of expectation that may prove too heavy for a girl's slim shoulders to bear. Mohini knows only her own expectations. If she can simply "love and be loved" she will be able to "remake her ideas and her outlook and all would be well." How can she yet know of Jayadev's dream of making her into the intellectual Vedic woman? Above all, how can she know of the curse lying over this house that only she can dispel?

Vedic learning, love, motherhood, a link between the old and the new—all these are expected of the girl Mohini as she enters Behula village.

Dominating the village is the Big House "on which time had left a smudged finger-mark." And dominating the Big House has been the Mother, widowed at twenty-five and from that time carrying on the traditions of family, caste, religion, culture.

In the first days Mohini is given the keys to the household safe and is shown the family tree. "My son's genealogy," the mother-in-law explains. "The last seventeen generations. The record of a thousand years." (123) Mohini, who has never seen more than five rupees at a time and who has no family tree of her own, now walks "loaded with responsibility."

Beyond the Big House Mohini gradually becomes acquainted with the village and its people. Her days are crowded with attempts at Vedic studies, household supervision, sewing for the longed-for son, worship at the father's shrine, temple visits, occasional chatter with the young women of her caste, who had at first found her city dress and ways so amusing. There is little time now for idle reading, and the gay voice and accompanying *dilruba* are muted, for modern secular songs are unwelcome to the Mother's ears.

But Jayadev's attempts to mold Mohini into the Maitreyi of 3,000 years ago prove abortive. Their companionship over the Sanskrit tomes is ended and Mohini begins to recognize her husband's quiet and reserved nature. The marital relationship becomes actively strained as Jayadev shifts his teachings to the Brahmin orphan girl, Sudha, whom his mother had instructed earlier.

V *Sudha and Others*

Sudha may be seen as the co-protagonist of the Mohini story— the dark shadow of Mohini's sun. Her blighted life pulls at the heartstrings of the reader and of Mohini, as well, even though Sudha is the Iago of her marriage.

At the age of fifteen and at the very altar of marriage, the beautiful and precocious Sudha had been declared by her guardian uncle to be under the evil eye of Saturn. Once postponed, the marriage never took place, or any other thereafter for Sudha. Eventually the unhappy girl had been brought to the Big House where the Mother helped to tutor her agile mind.

Sudha's dream of marriage to Jayadev was shattered by her inauspicious past, and the situation had been ripe for Sudha's hate when Mohini arrived as Jayadev's bride.

Sudha's shadow falls constantly across Mohini's life, and her name comes up again and again, sounding like a threatening tocsin. From the beginning Mohini has sensed Sudha's antagonism, but it is years before she recognizes its full import. And she will never know how near Sudha comes to replacing her in the marriage bed. So vividly is Sudha portrayed as Mohini's evil alter ego that one critic viewed her as the only character in the novel to come close to vying with the heroine in interest.

An opposing ray to Sudha's dark influence, however, is the young Ranjan who becomes Mohini's outlet for love and play. The eight-year-old relative of the family is taken in by Jayadev when he is left parentless. Immediately, he replaces Mohini's brother in her life. In this relationship there need be no artificial restraints, no prescribed formalities.

Another relationship is similarly uninhibited and helps to strengthen the bonds between husband and wife. Returned to the village is Harindra, a young surgeon whose father has been the village *kabiraj* of the traditional school of medicine. Harindra and his father represent in the world of medicine the same opposition of old and new that Jayadev and his mother represent in the general social and cultural scene.

But Jayadev and Harindra form a natural alliance for moving Behula into the modern world and for striving, at the village level, toward self-determination and self-respect for India herself. Harindra is the catalyst that fuses Jayadev's love of India's glorious past with a latent concern for her present and future. Jayadev comes to realize, "Thought had to be related to action. Abstraction had to be resolved in human terms." (169)

Associated with Jayadev and Harindra is a group of educated young men who have been pressing for village reforms and who look to the Big House for leadership. Of all their proposed reforms, the one most threatening to Behula village is that which would clean the temple tank from its rank overgrowth of water hyacinths as a major step in the battle against the mosquito. For every villager knows the thick mat of plants shelters and feeds a crocodile god that has lived at the bottom of the tank for generations. How the tank is eventually drained and the god proved nonexistent is one of the crisis points of the novel. In the face of human exigency in the episode of the pond, modern science and ancient belief resolve their differences.

VI *Motherhood*

In the meantime, Mohini and her mother-in-law are consumed by their mutual desire for a son and heir. Two years of marriage and still no sign of new life!

A joyous expectation of pregnancy proved false. Now Mohini is convinced she is barren. The mother-in-law, sharing that conviction, moves to the exploration of every ancient ritual and device, carrying the reluctant Mohini with her. A final resort is to the virgin goddess whose favorable intercession demands blood-letting from the petitioner's breast. Every fibre of Mohini's being rebels:

A brooding conflict was growing inside her. Opposite influences clutched her. Her enlightened girlhood was still a part of her fibre. She heard a voice as though her father were speaking.
"Have courage," it said. "Do not bow down to such insult. You are the New India. The old orthodox ways have been our yoke, have enslaved us. Let us be free."
And Old Mother's thin lips trembled as Mohini imagined her answer.
"How can we live without our past? Time is our earth, the earth which feeds our roots. Faith will not be denied. Give yourself to the goddess with grace, if not with faith." (204)

Mohini determines to make the blood offering with grace, leaving to her mother-in-law the act of faith.

An unlikely intercession comes in the form of Sudha, whom the Mother has seen as a logical and fruitful successor to Mohini if even the virgin goddess should prove unresponsive. In a confrontation at the very altar of the goddess, Mother and son declare their basic oppositions. "Heresy holds you. Old beliefs, old morals, old values mean nothing to you," cries the Mother. "For what sins in my past lives am I now punished?" To which the son replies, "Let's not be terrified by what seems to you inevitable. Are we not greater than our *karma*?" (221)

At the height of the tension, Mohini is found to be pregnant and though the son is not yet born, Mohini's crisis years are resolved on so happy a note the reader cannot doubt that Jayadev's savior and a new force for India will issue from the new woman that is Mohini.

On the eve of leaving for her first visit home since her marriage Mohini realizes she has become one with the village: "At home . . . she would not be truly away. The Big House lived in her, a part of her inmost self. At last, there was no discord. Life was music . . . her life was music—the true quest of every woman, her deepest need." (232)

And Sudha? Waiting in the wings for her is Harindra, the symbol of an emancipated India, ready to defy caste rules and marry the rejected Brahmin girl.

The conclusion of the story is somewhat ambiguous. Is Mohini's marriage now firmly established, or, in her absence, will Sudha reassert her hold over Jayadev? Bhattacharya has said he intended the book to conclude on this note. "I like to let the characters vanish into life," he once said. "Let the reader use his own imagination and write his own destiny for the characters."[2]

VII *Structual Balance and Harmony*

As with all his novels, Bhattacharya has an underlying social purpose in *Music for Mohini*. When independence is realized, how will India enter the future? Will she be able to throw off the shackles of ancient superstition and stultifying inhibitions to face the challenges of a new world? Jayadev finds the answer in a return to the most ancient Vedic past, infused with the energy and freedom of the present:

Society, rural society (and nine-tenths of India was rural) was sick with taboos and inhibitions of its own making: the iniquities of caste and untouchability; the ritualism that passed for religion; the wide-flung cobweb of superstitious faith. It was all an outgrowth of centuries of decadence. The purity of ancient thought had been lost in misinterpretation until the dignity of man had become a mere plaything of vested interest. Jayadev would break the crust of vulgarity and reveal ancient thought in its true splendor. But the new man of his vision, growing to his full stature, was not to be a hollow reincarnation, not a spiritless copy of ancient Hindu man. That were as stupid as the Hindu moulded in a Western pattern.

The freedom he envisioned must release a spiritual energy among the masses which would require every social value to be reweighed. This was the moment to end all slavery, not least of all the slavery of the spirit. The proud nation that would soon step onto the world stage could not afford to be half-slave, half-free. (80)

The incidents and the characters of the novel represent the conflicts between past and present and the need to achieve a balance and harmony if India is to survive.

Marjorie B. Snyder, writing in *The Chicago Tribune* (August 10, 1952), finds modern India revealed in *Music for Mohini* as "a sociological battleground in which the older generation clings to tradition ... [while] the intellectuals ... are struggling to throw away charms and bangles, to open themselves and their country to western ideas."

It seems that as the author achieves balance and harmony in the social scene and in Mohini's life, he demonstrates these elements in the structure of his novel. One is much more aware of formal structure in *Music for Mohini* than in other Bhattacharya novels—yet not disturbingly so. Questioned on this point during a conversation in 1971 in Honolulu, Bhattacharya pondered a moment and then conceded that "perhaps Mohini was more consciously structured than the other novels because it was set aside for a time and then returned to."

The book seems to fall naturally into two parts, each with similar structure and similar balances of characters and incidents, both achieving harmony and symmetry for the entire work.

Part I, in the Calcutta setting, presents the young Mohini in her warm home relationships (pages 1–74). Traditional India and the old forces are present in Mohini's grandmother. Her father is the bridge of transition between old and new. Mohini herself holds the promise of a creative and joyous future. Bindu, the "Cobra Maid," personalizes the dark forces that threaten Mohini's happiness, whereas the young brother, Heeralal, is the light and joy of her world. The other lesser figures in Mohini's life are given well-rounded characterizations that enlist the reader's sympathies.

The trip by train, bullock cart, and ancient palanquin from Calcutta to Behula afford a transitional link, or interlude, between the two parts (pages 75–98). As was said earlier, the stages of the journey, with their different modes of transportation, effectively symbolize the levels of life that separate the new India from the old.

Part II (pages 98–233) has to do with the village of Behula in which the Big House and Jayadev's mother are masterful physical representations of the psychological and social forces of traditional India. Here Jayadev is the transitional ground—more consciously so than was Father in Calcutta and hence more subject to doubt and ambivalence. His physician friend, Harindra, becomes his voice and his conscious motivation—an element not found in Part I. Sudha is the incarnation of the evil forces directed against Mohini in her new life, as the less articulate Bindu was in the old. And the young boy Ranjan replaces brother Heeralal as the affirmation of light and carefree joy.

In addition, the final portion of the novel is dominated by the metaphor of the village tank representing Behula itself. As the tank is choked with water hyacinths, at once beautiful and rank, so has village life been stultified by India's past. And Behula has its own "monster" in the form of unreasoning superstition. To be life-sustaining, the pool must be rid of its rank growth and crocodile; so, too, must the village be freed from blind adherence to the past and to superstitious fears.

The novel achieves a formal structure and balance through characterization, thus:

Part I—Calcutta	*Part II—Behula*
Mohini—young, innocent, romantic.	*Mohini*—maturing, acquiring new ideals, assuming new responsibilities.
Old Mother—Old India, guarding the traditions and passing them on to the young.	*The Mother*—Old India, rigorously bound to the past and harshly attempting to tie it to present and future.
Father—unconscious bridge between Old and New India; sometimes the conscious voice of the New.	*Jayadev*—self-declared bridge between Old and New India. *Harindra*—linked with Jayadev as the voice of New India.
Heeralal—carefree youth; the light and joy in Mohini's life.	*Ranjan*—the new light and joy of Mohini's life, whom she helps to free from earlier cares.
Bindu—personification of evil and the dark forces in Mohini's early world.	*Sudha*—the conscious spirit of evil and summation of the dark forces in Mohini's new world.

VIII *Articulation of the Social Message*

The author expresses his social philosophy most directly through the thoughts and words of Jayadev and of Harindra. At one point Jayadev muses:

Thought had to be related to action. Abstraction had to be resolved in human terms. The philosopher had to step out of his temple of silence and lead his people across the valley of conflict to end social slaveries.

> Social slaveries were cactus growths that would renew themselves over and again unless the roots were cut, roots that were deep in economic bondage. . . . A hungry man could not be free in spirit. (169–70)

Jayadev, however, is too much the scholar; too attracted to the idealized period of the far-distant Vedic Age to move easily into social reform. His philosophy needs a conscious agent to force it into action. As has been said, Harindra, the modern physician, is that agent. Bhattacharya, himself, once said (Honolulu, 1971): "Mohini expresses her action through life, not wittingly or philosophically. Harindra is the conscious, philosophical, and active expression of the future."

But it is in the life experiences of Mohini that the philosophy is brought into dramatic action, which is the stuff of which fiction is made. And it is through the refining fire of her experience that the dross is removed from the base metal of reform to produce the precious element of which the future will be wrought—an element that will weld the best of the past with the best of the future and from which the weakening impurities of blind superstition and bitter recrimination have been removed.

This is the resolution Bhattacharya sees as the salvation of contemporary India and the promise for her future—the synthesis or balance of East and West; a present and a future firmly based upon the cultural verities of the past. It is not by a renunciation of all that went before that the nation will prosper and her people realize lives of happiness and value. The final happy resolution for Mohini does not come with her shattering the shackles of tradition, with her leaving forever the backwash of the village for the burgeoning city. Whether knowingly or not, she is the shuttle that will weave together into one indivisible whole cloth the past and the future, the traditions of East and West, the values of village and city. She has responded to the heart of her mother-in-law as heard in her cry, "How can we live without our past?" She has responded also to the mind of her father, as in her imagination she heard him say, "You are the New India."

Bhattacharya points out that music is both a literal part of the book and used symbolically throughout the story. Therefore, he withdrew the manuscript from the first publisher to whom it had been submitted, in the face of the publisher's insistence that the title and the last page should be changed. Mohini struggles, the author says, "to make harmony of the discordant elements in her own life." But, on the broader scale, harmony must be established between the old and the new ways of life, between East and West. As Mohini has to adjust to strange village customs, so Jayadev's sister Roop-lekha had to enter the bewildering world of the city. To Mohini's suggestion that village-city intermarriage may be wrong since it certainly is accompanied by much unhappiness, Roop-lekha replies: "We who're so wed serve some real purpose. It's as though we made a bridge between two banks of a river. We connect culture with culture, Mohini, our old Eastern view of life with the new semi-Western outlook. . . . This is more urgent today than ever before. Our new India must rest on this foundation." (113)

And Roop-lekha sees Jayadev as performing a similar function: "You see, the New Learning holds him as much as the old, so that his heart is set on a synthesis, as he calls it. He would have a harmony of cultures for India. He reads ancient thought in today's light. He seeks in ancient thought sanction for the West-influenced ideals of our time. And he finds it. He is a man with a message for his country." (114)

Nevertheless, as was said at the outset, despite the weight of its social message, *Music for Mohini* has a life of its own as a creative fictional work. The lighthearted spirit of Mohini cannot be dimmed entirely by the national and social forces in which she is caught. To be sure, she ripens and matures as head of a large household, as wife, daughter-in-law, self-appointed teacher, and as expectant mother. But a spark of the irrepressible girl remains. Surely, the romantic Calcutta maiden become young village matron, is one of Bhattacharya's most appealing and most successful creations.

There is evidence that readers around the world have responded to the appeal of Bhattacharya's second novel. A *Chicago Tribune* review terms it "a splendid novel that may take rank with Pearl Buck's *The Good Earth*," and the *Cleveland News* judged it "one of the year's distinguished works of fiction." Millen Brand, who had edited all Bhattacharya's later novels for publication by Crown Publishers, New York, still regards *Music for Mohini* as his favorite and has referred to the "pure music" of the book. Most practical approval has come from France and Spain, however, where *Mohini*, soon after publication in translation there, was a book society selection.

CHAPTER 5

He Who Rides A Tiger

I Tiger *and* Hungers

*H*E *Who Rides a Tiger* presents provocative comparisons and contrasts with *So Many Hungers!* The world situation and the Indian dilemma are identical. World War II has entered its darkest days for Britain and her allies. The Japanese fleet is in the Bay of Bengal; Japanese bombers are making periodic forays over the sub-continent. What the forces from without may not be able to do, those from within are making the first really concerted effort to accomplish—the overthrow of the British Empire, with the resultant liberation of India.

India's strength is being vitiated, however, by casteism and greed. Famine, destitution, and displacement are ravaging the common people—not because of the forces of nature, but because of the rapacity of some men.

We can see, then, that the times and the circumstances are identical with those that are the background for *So Many Hungers!* However, the style and the focus of *He Who Rides a Tiger* make a very different book, indeed.

In the first place, Bhattacharya is much more the master of his medium than he was in *So Many Hungers!* The writing style is smoother and more consistent; it has lost the somewhat disturbing derivative overtones of the first novel. Characterization, also, is more even, the residents of the great city being presented with as much warmth and empathy as those of the village.

Secondly, the situation or focus differs from that of the earlier account. Whereas *So Many Hungers!* condemns chiefly the land-owners, merchants, and big businessmen for their exploitation of the impoverished, powerless, and uneducated peasantry, *He Who Rides a Tiger* centers on the evils of caste and superstitious religion. These

twin evils are relentlessly castigated, but without the bitterness that
runs through *So Many Hungers!* (The first novel "had to be bitter,"
Bhattacharya once said. "It was the human scene that made me a
novelist.")

According to Bhattacharya, while *So Many Hungers!* is a "straight
story," *He Who Rides a Tiger* is a satire. It is more concerned with
human problems in general. In fact, the way in which the problems
of deprivation and exploitation are revealed and attacked contains
much ironic humor. Also, although Nationalism sounds a recurring
note in this new treatment of the World War II theme, it is not the
central motif that it is in the earlier book.

II   *Father and Daughter*

The crude but intelligent Kalo, a blacksmith in the village of
Jharna, centers his life on his beautiful daughter, Chandra Lekha.
He finds in her a reincarnation of her mother, who left the world as
her child entered. He is awed that a man such as he should have so
gentle and lovely a child. And there is prescience in the naming of the
girl. When the child's birth was imminent, a Brahmin priest, who
was patronizing Kalo in his shop, suggested that if the child were a
boy he should be named Obhijit, if a girl, Chandra Lekha, the Moon-
tinted One. So it came about that the simple Kamar's child received
an acceptable Brahmin name.

In Kalo's mind nothing can be too good for Lekha. She attends
the village mission school as though she were highborn, soon estab-
lishing herself as first in her class. And so that he will not appear
ignorant in her eyes, Kalo begins teaching himself late at night,
studying the mission books by flickering lamplight. Lekha's school
career ends in what should have been a blaze of glory. Perhaps pre-
sumptuously, in her final year she enters a state-wide essay contest
for the Ashoka literary prize—and wins! The first girl ever to receive
the coveted silver medal. But though a review and picture appear
in the city paper, the townsfolk make no mention of the honor. The
hurt leaves a psychological scar which Kalo will bear the remainder
of his life.

Three years later—in 1943—a hunger plague strikes Bengal in the
wake of war. The innocent and idyllic life in the village is shattered.
Kalo sits idly; there is no work and no pay for a smithy in times like
these. Land, goods, working tools are being sold in order to buy

rice at exhorbitant prices from the city profiteers. Jharna is now a ghost town. Kalo holds on longer than many others, living off his meager savings. But the day comes when he must go to Calcutta. Lekha is left with an old aunt until Kalo is able to send for her.

An ill-fated moment during Kalo's trip to the city results in a brief but decisive term in jail during which he is advised by a young inmate that when he gets to the big city he should either enter Lekha into a house of prostitution or assume the role of mendicant priest and earn their livelihood by begging. The advice soon takes on the guise of prophecy fulfilled.

Despite his struggles against fate, Kalo eventually becomes the procurer for several whorehouses in one of which—much in the tradition of old-time melodrama—he comes upon a terrified Lekha and rescues her.

Father and daughter are at last reunited. But Kalo is without employment in a hostile city. What to do? He recalls the suggestion of his young cellmate and determines to pose as a Brahmin priest. He thinks of it not only as a means to earn a living, but as a way to "hit back" at the society that has oppressed them. The future is determined.

III   *From Kamar to Brahmin*

The scene shifts to a roadside on the outskirts of the city where we find an unknown holy man the center of a curious gathering.

Shiva's coming. That was the occasion, sponsored by a tall, dark, big-built Brahmin in a holy man's yellow cloak and skull cap, a rosary on his neck. He sat with his legs crossed on a striped tiger skin spread under the banyan, and tirelessly, in a sonorous tone, he spoke the charmed words "Namo Shivaya" which his listeners solemnly echoed. He swayed to the words and stooped now and then to pour a little water on the ground out of a brass pitcher. Close by, on another tiger skin, sat a girl, and she, too, was dressed in yellow; her long rich hair flowing down her back and arms, her fair brow thickly smeared with vermilion. But her voice, as one heard it below the chanting chorus, rang hollow; her face was curiously rigid; her hands, helping with the brass pitcher, were puppet hands worked by strings. (77)[1]

The priest is, of course, Kalo who has entered upon a new way of life. As the "Brahmin," Mangal Adhikari, the former smith finds himself successful beyond his wildest dreams. Before long a temple rises at the site of a miraculous manifestation, and the wealthiest and highest born men of the city are vying with one another for the honor and "merit" of giving.

Kalo's crossing of caste barriers was now complete; it had been accepted without a question, but the sacrilege had not been easy for him:

Kalo twisted his sacred thread to his thumb, in Brahminic manner, seeking his strength from the contact, and let his trembling hand rest upon his stomach.

It was a thick, brand-new thread with nine white strands, no simple thread but a Brahmin's holy emblem. Putting it on had involved a moral struggle. The terrible fraud of posing as high of caste, the highest, when he was so far down in the scale. No man in Bengal could ever before have dared such rashness. Doubt preyed on his mind. Where would this end? . . .

On the crossroads of his life Kalo had sat in bewildered brooding. How to keep up the awful masquerade without stumbling, without betraying himself?

"What other way?" The voice of the rebel in him was grim with the desperation which came out of the bowels of Bengal.

He had closed his eyes. He had held his breath. Clutching the sacred thread in his hands he had passed it swiftly over his shoulder and across his bare chest. The daring of that gesture made him tremble. With that gesture he had thrown off the heavy yoke of his past and flouted the three thousand years of his yesterdays. Putting on the sacred thread he had made himself rootless.

The terror of that act was followed by a deep sense of release. He had transcended the station that birth and blood had assigned him. Exhilaration and new courage filled him. (80–81)

Not only is the temple well financed, but money and jewels and food are showered on Kalo and Lekha. The new life is launched, there is no turning back: "He rode a lie as if it were a tiger, which he could not dismount lest the tiger pounce upon him and eat him up." (84)

As he puts doubt and hesitation aside, the simple blacksmith recognizes a certain fated irony in his new role:

Han, that was the way to avenge himself. A smith reincarnated a Brahmin. A convict and harlot-house procurer become a master of a temple, placing the hand of benediction on the bowed heads of pious folk. So had the Wheel of Karma turned! (85)

Kalo sees it in his power to rule the present and future lives of those who had wronged him. Their every act of devotion, performed

at the unsanctified temple under the guidance of a non-Brahmin
"priest" would mire them in iniquity. The more devout they were,
the more damned! Kalo comes to see himself as an avenging instrument. All who falsely worship Shiva through him are doomed;
therefore, the entire system of traditional belief is destroyed because
of him. If he is to be truly effective, however, his sphere must
broaden.

This was not going to be the sole false Shiva in the great city. Others must be
installed, and true temples put into shade by the false ones with their aggressive
splendour. (112)

He will prove to all that religious form and ritual are hollow, ex-
isting for the appeasement of rich and poor alike—for the con-
sciences of the rich and the sufferings of the poor.

IV *Change*

The old, simple faith of his village life is gone. Where? Why?
Adversity had destroyed it. He no longer believed in the established
forms and ancient traditions he had once accepted without question.
Yet—oddly enough—he found himself concerned about the results
of his evil deeds, not the least of which were those in which he was
now involved. "It may be that your fellowmen won't find you out
and punish you," he said to himself. "But how will you get away
from your karma? All that you do in this life goes to make the
writing on your brow in the lives to come." (117)

Significantly, the instrument of Kalo's salvation is a man whom
he has taken to work in the temple gardens—Viswanath, another
former blacksmith, who may be seen as Kalo's true self. Viswanath
had been rescued from starvation by Kalo and had accepted with
gratitude the humble work about the temple grounds, but without
losing his air of dignity and independence. Both are asserted in
dramatic action when it is discovered that the old gardener is
taking the temple's ritual milk to feed destitute babies. When the
sacrilege is reported to Kalo, he supports Viswanath rather than
tradition.

Kalo realizes this may be the act that will end his brief "incarnation" as a Brahmin priest. But within him a feeling of honest justice
has been aroused. By a masterly playing off of one self-interest

against another, Kalo manages to have the sacred milk continue to go to the "starveling ones."

The forces of social concern, once awakened in Kalo, gradually grow stronger. He will never again be able to return to the narrow and bitter course of personal revenge that had dominated his life during the months in the great city.

Contributing factors come apace: the release of Kalo's fellow prisoner, Biten, from jail and his addition to the temple community; hunger marches with Nationalist overtones that periodically pass the temple and in which Viswanath and Biten participate; and, finally, Lekha's bringing into the family a small starving boy she has found on the street.

Reluctantly, Kalo is forced out of his preoccupation with self and plunged into concern for others and for India herself. There are two final determining factors. One is the discovery that Biten is actually Bikash Mukerji, a Brahmin who has rejected his privileged status to live humbly and to give himself to the impoverished and to national liberation. Food for thought—that this vital young man should reject the very thing Kalo has exerted himself to acquire. The other factor is the love the orphan child arouses in Kalo's heart. Once more a small life is dependent upon him and has faith in him, trusts him implicitly. How can he continue to live a life of deceit before Obhijit, as he names this long-delayed "son"?

V *The Reckoning*

But as Kalo's life begins to turn back from deception, ironically Lekha, who had been the unwilling collaborator, finds herself entangled in a new mesh of circumstance which results in her becoming the "Mother of Sevenfold Bliss," an object of temple worship and the expected source of miracles.

She, like Kalo before her, comes eventually to enjoy the adulation and almost to believe in her own divinity. But she is released from her sainthood with cruel abruptness through the death of a child whom she is assumed to have healed. Lekha's inner eyes are reopened to the truth of her common humanity and she joins her father on the road back to honest identity.

One final involvement in human relationships remains to be solved, however, as Lekha struggles between the desires of her heart and the temptations of wealth. Her decision to sacrifice herself in a loveless marriage in order to secure the temple leadership for her father, is the ultimate self-revelation for Kalo.

With a masterful denouement, the author, in a final fast-moving chapter, resolves the remaining questions and conflicts.

At a temple ceremony to install Lekha formally as the temple goddess (soon to be abruptly annulled by her impending marriage) Kalo steps out of the charade. Lekha's self-sacrifice has been the final decisive factor.

He was riding a tiger and could not dismount. He had sat astraddle, half-resigned but helpless, while the beast prowled or raced at will. Yet even as he rode, he had been aware all the time that there was no way but to kill the tiger.

The idea of giving up ease, comfort, security for the hard living in Jharna town had frightened him. It had made him feel feeble and his legs had pressed against the flanks of his mount, tightening his seat.

But the need to kill the tiger grew because of a strength in him, a strength he had never known before. It was the strength which comes of seeing people as they are. . . . (226)

So here, before the mass gathering, Kalo reveals himself for what he is: no Brahmin priest, but a simple village Kamar driven by hardship and injustice. The crowd sits stunned, "in the grip of shock"—Chandra Lekha, as well. There are a variety of reactions, but Chandra Lekha responds with sheer worship. Here is the father she knew, honored, and loved, returned from a far-off and strange place with strength renewed.

Significantly, in the novel's concluding scene Kalo has won the allegiance of the masses of the people and stands supported by the Brahmin, Bikash Mukerji, and the Sudra, Viswanath, as he faces an uncertain future with honesty and courage.

VI *Critical Response*

Bhattacharya's third novel, *He Who Rides a Tiger*, is considered by many to be the high-water mark in his career, his "masterpiece." I am inclined to this belief myself, although I admit to some bias, perhaps. For I came upon *Tiger* in a Madras bookstore not too long after its publication, and it is the only Bhattacharya book I have read in the Indian setting. With the sights, sounds, and people of India about me, the story and its characters seemed obviously genuine and the situations sincere. The novel spoke to me with the affirmation of the home source.

One scholar, evaluating the novel in terms of the *rasa* ("flavor," "relish," "esthetic taste") theory enunciated in early Sanskrit criticism, sees the novel as a "dramatic illustration" of the type of work recognized by classical critics as a "type of *rasa*-inspired art work . . . in which the *rasa* itself is subordinated to an 'objective factor,' a content or message." From this base he finds Bhattacharya's "philosophical position impeccable."[2] But *He Who Rides a Tiger* apparently has spoken eloquently to readers in any setting. It has received enthusiastic acclaim in some of the most respected Western publications. Orville Prescott wrote in *The New York Times*:

> Bhabani Bhattacharya writes of Indians and the social, cultural and religious world in which they live with an authority and understanding that no Western writer could hope to match. And he writes with complete mastery of the fictional technique of the West. His English prose is smooth and supple. *He Who Rides a Tiger* is a skillful and entertaining story and an illuminating glimpse inside one corner of India. But it is more than that. Its indignation is warm and generous; its material is fresh; its writing blessed with vigor and charm.

The Times of London: "This is a rare and beautiful novel." And *The Sunday Times* (London): "The book crystallizes with compassion and understanding the heart and the tragedy of India."

Joseph Hitrec in *The Saturday Review* centered his evaluation on the core of Bhattacharya's philosophy as a writer, judging the value of a creative work in terms of its effectiveness as an instrument of social concern. Calling *Tiger* "a moral tale," Mr. Hitrec commented:

> Bhattacharya's writing craft is clearly a product of the same fermenting forces that have shaped his moral viewpoint. The pronounced moralizing note evident throughout the novel precludes him from being a realistic writer in our sense. But social though his theme is he is yet not a tendentious writer. His style and attitude might have a resemblance to the early Upton Sinclair except for a quality of incantation that goes straight back to the scriptural poetry of the Hindus, and from which Bhattacharya is still trying to free himself. One can only hope that he will for he has important things to say about his country and his people and he has his heart in the right place.

Some of the early Upton Sinclair may be here, but the Indian author lacks the abrasiveness of Sinclair. Admittedly, the novel carries a weight of social criticism, but the treatment has little of the polemics to be found in Sinclair or, for that matter, in the earlier *So Many Hungers!* The irony that runs throughout is relieved by subtle humor and a warm empathy for the human condition.

More importantly, however, I would strongly disagree with Hitrec's objection to what he calls Bhattacharya's "quality of incantation." (Compare this with Prescott's comment on Bhattacharya's "complete mastery of the fictional technique of the West," quoted above.) Why should he "free himself" from a truly indigenous quality in his writing style? It seems to me that one of the major dividends in delight that comes with reading works written in English but arising from other cultures is the sense one gets of a heretofore unrecognized use to which the mundane language of daily commerce can be put. Why should not Bhattacharya's English prose assume a different tone, a different color, from that of Joseph Hitrec? And why can it not speak to us despite this metamorphosis? Need we assume Bhattacharya's "important things" are not said to those of us who are born to the English tongue because his English is enriched by the qualities of the magnificent "scriptural poetry of the Hindus"? I should hope not. Indeed, his message seems to have got across to Hitrec, himself![3]

VII *The Characters*

Even more than in the earlier novels, characters are complex, torn by competing loyalties, precariously balanced between antagonistic forces within and without. Bhattacharya is masterful in depicting the response of characters to stress. Under the force of circumstances Kalo gradually shifts from the gentle, warmhearted, genuine man he was in the happy years of Chandra Lekha's childhood in the village. The first thorn of disappointment comes when his fellow villagers disregard Lekha's winning of the Ashoka prize. This festers within his subconsciousness, beginning to throb again with each new strain that is put upon him. To the objective observer, a small thing. To the doting parent, how real!

From the prison months Kalo emerges with a more realistic view of life, and it is not long before the big city has destroyed completely the illusions with which he had set out from home. The exigencies of destitution and hunger that led to his employment in the prostitution "trade" finally harden a previously gentle character to the point where Kalo is ready to live in duplicity, cynically taking advantage of the gullibility of the poor and the hypocrisy of the wealthy.

Yet there seems no inconsistency in the ultimate reassertion of Kalo's finer qualities, as his eyes are opened again to the suffering about him and as he becomes aware of the ultimate sacrifice being made by Chandra Lekha. We recognize that Kalo's essential character has remained constant even when it was worked upon by the negative forces of the times in which he lived.

Lekha, too, has her weaknesses as well as her strengths. She who had condemned her father for coming to enjoy and even believe in his false Brahminhood finds herself beginning to take pleasure in her role as sacred *devi* of the spurious temple. But at the conclusion her devotion to her father and to the age-old verities by which she lived in the village is reasserted, and we find the true Chandra Lekha restored and strengthened by the testing of her character.

We have no sense here—as we have in *So Many Hungers!*—that one of the characters may be largely autobiographical; although, to a certain extent, the disaffected Bikash Mukerji may be the author. Bikash, Kalo, and Viswanath are all voices of Bhattacharya's social philosophy. Here is the author speaking as Kalo tells Lekha about his prison experience:

> . . . One thing I do not understand, Chandra Lekha. The idea is to reform the convict, make him a better man, is it not? But they do their utmost to make the convict feel he is not human at all. . . . His human dignity is put between grindstones until it turns to powder and blows away. . . . Day by day the convict loses his fear. Day by day he gathers hate inside him, so it fills him altogether. Hate, not for the wardens alone, hate, for the system that creates such wardens. Hate for everything. It becomes an illness of the mind. (107–108)

And Bikash, talking with Kalo in prison, speaks with bitterness of the thriving trade in prostitutes, asking why women, alone, should "suffer so much from social tyranny." It is Bikash who first gives voice to the injustices in the caste system and who, himself, rejects his caste. It is Bikash, again, who sees all men as his brothers and who strives for a free and independent India. The characters of Kalo, Bikash, and Viswanath merge and become one in the character of the author himself.

VIII   *Universal Appeal*

In Russia alone *He Who Rides a Tiger* is said to have sold some 90,000 copies. One can see the basis for its appeal, not only there but in diverse cultures and languages. For there is universality in this story which, in its telling, combines warmth of human understanding, concern for the inequities of the social order, and a sense of the dignity of common life.

CHAPTER 6

A Goddess Named Gold

I *Multiplicity of Purpose*

DESPITE its deceptive fairy-tale quality and the humor that pervades the story, *A Goddess Named Gold* carries perhaps a greater weight of purpose than any other Bhattacharya novel. At one point the reader may conclude the author is chiefly concerned in attacking the evils of unadulterated greed, or of blackmarket profiteering; at another, in asserting women's worth. Or the purpose might be to raise the question of India's uncertain future as she achieves nationhood. Or, how will the universal franchise operate in a largely illiterate citizenry?

Actually, each of these concerns surfaces again and again to be dealt with in a variety of ways, but more often than not with revealing satire. Samsundar, "the Seth" or great merchant, is a veritable Micawber transplanted from the streets of Dickensian London to a dusty village in Bengal. Like Micawber, he dresses ostentatiously in a style befitting what he considers to be his exalted position:

> [At his office desk the Seth] had a yellow turban on his head and his stocky figure was oddly draped in a bathrobe of blue-and-mauve toweling, ankle-length. The unusual garb gave him an air of sophistication. Awe-struck eyes would gape at the large, blue buttons and silken tassel with its smart loop. The Seth was known to possess a half-dozen costumes of this kind in different colors, all purchased, it was said, at an English store in Bombay, the great city five hundred miles away, where the Seth had gone twice on business trips.
>
> A parasol stood in a corner. . . . [It] also had come from Bombay. Its yellow silk had wide green bands and the small squat handle was highly polished. The people of Sonamitti had seen no other umbrella of this kind; like the bathgown it was an item of dignity in the Seth's outfit, an insignia of prestige.

He had to be careful about its use, however. The delicate silk could not be exposed to sun and rain and wind. (37–38)[1]

Around the Seth swirls action both serious and ridiculous. His dreams of personal glory and fortune, like Mr. Micawber's, are invariably aborted at the moment of birth. Though the Seth has a potential for evil beyond the talent of his English prototype, a man so bumbling, so inept, and so downright funny the reader cannot either detest or reject. Most of the gut-level humor in *A Goddess Named Gold* involves this ubiquitous and irrepressible character.

Lines of good and evil in the village of Sonamitti are drawn initially between the women on one side and the men on the other. "The Cowhouse Five," who meet daily in the Seth's cowshed for two hours every mid-day when the rest of the village sleeps, are led by the beautiful young Meera and her grandmother into one action after another that pit the women against the men, who are led by the Seth. Yet, true to Bhattacharya's usual balanced view, not all women can be seen as good, all men as evil. One reviewer of *A Goddess Named Gold* made a strong point of Bhattacharya's avoidance of character stereotyping, saying: "All of Bhattacharya's people come alive; each is a mixture of good and bad, of wisdom and foolishness."[2] Another, saying "it is hardly possible to overpraise this novel," found in it "many characters the ordinary visitor to India would never know existed, creating the community spirit which everywhere binds the pure against evil."[3]

The very fact that the women congregate at siesta time, however, stamps them as activists. Even the greedy Seth—too active in his own behalf—retires during the heat of the day. In drawing the lines so clearly here, with the women indefatigable in behalf of good, and clear-sighted in their purposefulness, while the Seth muddles his logic, advances and retreats, Bhattacharya seems to assert the ultimate, inevitable triumph of good over evil.

As the novel opens, the Cowhouse Five are reviewing with satisfaction their previous activity to help achieve India's independence from England. Meera's grandma is their hero, having once served a prison term in the freedom struggle. Now that independence is only a hundred days away, how will women participate in their nation's freedom, what will be their role, their "rights"? But, more immediately, how will they wrest from the Seth the cloth he has been hoarding the past months, awaiting the day when the demand will be so great that he will be able to sell it on his own stiff terms? The scene in which the women worst the Seth largely through the action of his own wife is the first of many side-splitting episodes. Ralph Block, writing in the *Washington Post* (August 21, 1960), found in this episode "aspects of the Lysistrata story coupled with the legend of Godiva."

II   *The Song-maker*

The women have won "the battle of the saris." Meera has rescued the Seth's only son from drowning. In petty retaliation against the victorious women, the Seth plans a free movie from which the women will be barred.

Back to a village that has become increasingly embroiled in its own trifling concerns, then, comes the Minstrel, Meera's grandfather, after three years wandering the countryside singing for the people the songs of India's great past, her demanding present, and her challenging future. Only the Minstrel can bring the perspective necessary to restore community order.

As Meera's grandfather tells her of his role in life we can hear Bhattacharya enunciating his own philosophy of the function of the poet—the writer—in society:

"He has to be above our petty battles. A song-maker must not live only for himself or his kith and kin. He has to carry a flame in his hand, passing it from age to age. Let him stumble and the flame will falter. Let him fall and there will be the chillness as of death." (63)

[Meera realizes that] he belonged not to her, not to Grandma, but to all the people; or else he would not be a true minstrel. The Grandpapa was lost in the song-maker. Looking at him with worship in her eyes, she could almost see the flame held aloft in his hand, the flame handed to him from other song-makers, who reached far back through time, through the spaces of hundred-years, to a dim past when words were not written on paper or palm-leaf or tree bark, they had to be passed from mouth to mouth, memory to memory. (64)

Although the Minstrel remains above the "petty battles" of the village during his three-day visit, he alerts Meera, and, through her, the Cowhouse Five, to the responsibilities of citizenship in an independent nation. He also ultimately contributes the element about which will coalesce the destructive forces of selfishness and greed.

When her grandfather asks Meera the significance of the school-boys' marching through the village chanting, "Vote for Samsundarji, vote!", Meera replies unconcernedly that the Seth is anxious to sit on the District board and seeks the vote of the villagers.

> She asked, "What is this vote-mote?"
> He explained. Since India was to be free, the wheels of life would run henceforth under the power of the people's vote. Wheels of many kinds, big and small. . . .
> She nodded, crying, "I understand. No, no, the Seth cannot be our voice. Does he know our heart?"
> They were now close to the fig tree. A man was seen standing on the ve-randa—it was the Seth himself. "We will not let him go to the board-moard, Grandpapa," Meera said in a whisper.
> "You must not." (70–71)

For a time the Cowhouse Five promote Meera's grandmother as opposition candidate for the "board-moard." Later they turn to the young Meera, herself. Having been established as intelligent and energetic "prime movers" in the life of Sonamitti, the introduction of women as likely candidates for office in popular elections is readily accepted by the reader, as by the villagers—perhaps so well accepted, indeed, that there is some disappointment when the selection swings in another direction at the conclusion of the action. Nevertheless, the women of the village remain throughout the strongest motivating forces in all aspects of village life.

The selfishness and greed, epitomized in the character of the Seth, are sublimated in the general life of Sonamitti until the Minstrel performs an act that brings them to the surface where they can be exorcised. Cleansed, the village will be prepared to meet the dawn of a new India.

Before leaving the village, after an evening singing some of the episodes of the great *Ramayana*, the Minstrel ties to Meera's arm a *taveez*—a magic amulet. "This taveez holds a stone," he tells her. "The stone has power. It is a touchstone. . . . Wearing it on your person you will do an act of kindness. Real kindness. Then all copper on your body will turn to gold. . . . Gold with which to do good— . . . An act of real kindness—that is the key, remember." (85)

Miraculously, the amulet appears to assert its power immediately, for the gold-washed copper ring Meera has been wearing is found

to have been changed to pure gold. Only much later is it revealed
the Minstrel had caused the copper ring to be taken from Meera's
finger to be replaced by the gold. The loving grandfather had wanted
Meera to wear a ring of real value, but she had persisted in rejecting
it: "This copper, Grandpapa" [she had told him]. "With a gold
wash it looks good enough. Hard to understand why people hanker
for pure gold or at least silver." (74)

The substitution of real for simulation, however, has a deeper
purpose than the satisfying of an old man's fancy. Together with
the "magic" amulet it may inspire men like the Seth to do good
deeds.

III   *Subversion*

It does not take long for the Seth to see the *taveez* as a means
for his personal gain if he can but get Meera to concur in his wishes.
Through the best of intentions the girl, who by her inner nature
had acted in behalf of others, ultimately sells her magic power to
the Seth. Her slim body weighted down with copper coins given
her by the Seth and village friends, under the merchant's directions
she begins doing "acts of kindness" trumped up by the Seth without her knowledge. As her misery deepens so does the village sink,
day by day, into the mire of greed and dissatisfaction. Suspicion
gathers about her head, and the girl who once had been regarded
as the friend of all and the angel of the oppressed is gradually
ostracized and condemned.

Involvement follows involvement until the ultimate disillusion
of both Meera and the Seth in the power of the *taveez*. Finally,
Meera tears the amulet from her arm and casts it into the river when
she comes to realize that no good can come from putting "kindness
on sale." (Bhattacharya has called this scene "the key to the whole
book.") Even the Seth has grown to detest the domination the amulet has taken over his every motive and act:

> Obsessed by gold, he had let all his routine work slacken and stop. . . .
> And there was the district board, of course. So much remained to be done,
> and he was content to let his energy ooze down his fingertips. Time to set
> things right. Time for hard, honest donkey's work. (287)

The village women, who at first had besought Meera to change
their pitiful pice into precious gold and then had suspected her

integrity, submit themselves once more to the power of tradition. One of them sums up their single thought:

"How can we change the past thousand years of our living? A river has flown between the rich and the poor. There is no boat to take the poor to the other bank. The rich cross the stream at their will. They put wary feet on the mud and from a distance they hail the poor and speak good words and feel pleased with themselves that they have been so kind. It is a game for the rich to play. But the river flows on and the rich return to their bank and wash mud off their feet. And the river flows on." (256)

IV   *Redemption*

Part of the redemptive power in *A Goddess Named Gold* springs from the character of Sohanlal, the young man from the city who has been brought to Sonamitti by the Seth to serve as driver for his motorbike. With the handsome young "driver fellow" at the controls, the Seth returns to the village riding in the sidecar. Sonamitti's first motor vehicle has been purchased to assure the Seth's election to the "board-moard" and to be used for his "touring duty" following election.

All Sonamitti, every ass and owl and monkey, would have something to talk about when they saw the dart of red lightning on Main Road. Then they would know whom to vote for! (94)

Although Sohanlal, in his somewhat bemused association with the Seth, is partner to much of the slapstick fun in *A Goddess Named Gold*, he is also co-agent with the Minstrel in helping to move the townspeople into a future in which the India of the past will unite with the India of the future.

Sohanlal has his counterpart in other Bhattacharya novels: Prokash, Rahoul's politically active laboratory assistant in *So Many Hungers!*; Harindra, the Western-educated physician, in *Music for Mohini*; Biten, the Brahmin turned social reformer, in *He Who Rides a Tiger*; and, perhaps in more extreme terms, Bhashkar in *Shadow from Ladakh*.

Early in his life in the village Sohanlal is attracted to Meera, and he remains a steadying influence throughout her entanglement with the Seth and her struggles to reaffirm her natural yearning to do good for those about her. While the villagers—those who have known her intrinsic worth throughout a lifetime—turn against her, accusing her of using the *taveez* solely for her own profit—this stranger from the city has instant recognition of her purposes:

> How could he sense her inmost feeling? "The taveez belongs to your heart, Meera, do I not understand?" And as she stared at his face, seeking mockery, he went on, "The miracle is just the means. The purpose is all that counts. . . ."
> The rush of happiness made her breath quicken. Even though he had no faith in the touchstone, he understood her, he sympathized! (225)

Furthermore, Sohanlal joins other of Bhattacharya's socially aware characters as he acknowledges the value of women:

> Where is true union between man and woman unless they accept each other as equals? he was asking himself. You cannot worship and yet despise. It is the conceit in you that makes you despise. (225)

Sohanlal encourages Meera in the abandonment of the *taveez* but leaves the decision and resultant act to her. It is Sohanlal, also, who points the direction for the village's selection of the Minstrel as its first representative on the District board.

As in all Bhattacharya's novels-with-a-purpose, *A Goddess Named Gold* concludes with an affirmation of the basic decency of the human spirit. The village, which had gone mad over the promise of sudden, unearned wealth, breathes a mass sigh of relief when the ill-fated *taveez* is cast aside. After seven weeks of frenetic and misguided activity, all settle down to the serious business of facing the future as citizens in a free India. The Minstrel has returned and by mass acclamation is named candidate for the "board-moard." One has a sense that the Seth, too, feels relieved that his bid for office is not to be endorsed, thus freeing him for accomplishment more in keeping with his natural bent.

The men and women of Sonamitti have lived through the refiner's fire, have salvaged the precious metal from the dross of life, and face their future and the future of their new nation better prepared as a result of their experience. Honest work and consecrated purpose—no magic means—are what India needs from all her people. "A new hope was born. A truer touchstone was at everyone's grasp. . . . A touchstone that was freedom's gift for the people." (304) But a gift from freedom earned by lives in dedicated service to high ideals.

The "magic" stone given Meera by her grandfather, which may have seemed to have done more harm than good, has actually been the agent for purification and redemption. In his wisdom the Minstrel set the conditions by which the villagers will come to recognize life's real values, reaching the truth through their own actions rather than by means of his direct preachment. (Arrival at truth through human action is also the novelist's tool.) But, as the action concludes, the Minstrel points up a lesson for the assembled villagers— Freedom must be the touchstone, its miracle released when all work together in faith.

V   *"Tinkling Fable"* or *Complicated Composition?*

When *A Goddess Named Gold* first appeared in the summer of 1960 it was widely and enthusiastically reviewed. Critics variously termed it a "parable," a "fable," a "fairy tale." In *The New York Times Book Review* (August 21, 1960), Joseph Hitrec spoke of this fourth Bhattacharya novel as the author's typical combination of "tinkling fable of weakness, rural facts of life and pure fun—ingredients which Mr. Bhattacharya has made his own, and which, with a happy knack, he manages to blend into diverting stories with a moral."

Although "tinkling fable" may be present to a certain extent in Bhattacharya's earlier novels, with the possible exception of the highly fanciful *He Who Rides a Tiger*, they are, in general, more straightforward and realistic than is *A Goddess Named Gold*, which has an obvious load of moral preachment. I agree with Millen Brand, Bhattacharya's editor at Crown Publishers, that moral purpose need not necessarily be at odds with realism. Brand has said:

The life of India calls strongly for moral and social awareness, but I don't know that this is necessarily in conflict with realism. Realism is not literalism and has its own range, with even virtuoso strokes of the imagination. And so I would not like to see any hint of the perjorative in discussing realism as against moral writing. If the morality is true and based on truth, I see it in the admirable light of Gandhi's saying, "Bring truth to power."[4]

Rosanne Archer found the story a skillful blend of realism and romanticism. In *The New York Herald Tribune Book Review* (August 28, 1960) she commented on the book's lack of "astringency" and on "the compassion and insight" that accompany the considerable "romanticism."

Parable, fable, or fairy tale, *A Goddess Named Gold* apparently speaks directly to peoples of many cultures and many levels of sophistication, for it has been widely translated into other languages, bringing the book to readers in such diverse lands as Russia, China, Israel, and France. Also, the book has been required reading for Malaysian children in the schools of Kuala Lumpur.

Interestingly, the story's didactic shoe has been found to fit a variety of feet. Commenting on the novel in *Swarajya* (July 28, 1962), Prema Nandakumar opened her review by saying that "*A Goddess Named Gold* stands out as a novel with a purpose, sustained by high seriousness and alive with symbolism." She then equates the message with India's response to independence, achieved as the novel closes:

The "amulet" is the gift of freedom which Gandhiji and the band of brave warriors, who had stood with him in fair and foul weather alike, have made to us. But what are we making of this "freedom"? We have idealists like Meera among us, but there are the Seths, too, there are the ever-ready bureaucrats (the Bulaki Raos) who are willing to translate the whims of idealists and the schemes of the calculators into crude, ugly realities, be the cost to the mass of the people what it may. The rich are getting richer, the tribe of the bureaucrat is on the increase . . . Where are "acts of faith" in all-embracing Statism? Where are "acts of kindness" in a permit-license-quota-ridden regime? . . . We need faith in ourselves and in our fellow-men, we need the religion that we—the rich and the poor—are all members of one another, and we need the courage to rely on ourselves for our salvation. . . . We have, in short, to hearken to the minstrel-grandfather's words . . . "Remember, friends, all this cannot be cheaply won. The miracle will not drop upon us. It is we who have to create it with love and with sweat. Freedom is the means to that end."

A *Christian Science Monitor* critic finds a universal fit, writing: "Mr. Bhattacharya shows in this imaginatively conceived and brilliantly written story that the frantic scrambling for financial balance usually combines both comedy and tragedy."

Likewise, Joseph Hitrec recognizes universal dimensions. In *The New York Times Book Review* item, quoted earlier, he writes:

With a wagging finger, the author seems to argue that planned generosity—like planned parenthood—has its limitations, and he reminds us that the proposition was thrashed out and defined ages ago in the words of Bhagavad Gita: "Thou must do good without the thought of self." Organized kindness is tainted, and therefore no kindness. But since he loves the people he scolds and his fun-poking is without brittle edges, his lesson is pleasant to take.

Apparently American toes have also wriggled into the Indian sandal, the "didactic shoe," referred to earlier. Bhattacharya says that, after reading *A Goddess Named Gold*, an American diplomat asked whether he was not, in fact, speaking against American aid to India. Just money, he concluded, would not solve the problems of the village—"Life is not all that simple." In his conversation with me on this point Bhattacharya made an interesting transition by commenting on American aid to Pakistan. "Pakistan," he said, "has been fed on American money. But they have not developed their country as they might have done." Implying, if they had used their own dedication and resources to the full rather than depending so much on the "magic *taveez*" of American assistance things might have been different.

As has been said, *A Goddess Named Gold*, which at the opening may seem just a cut above froth and burlesque, before it has progressed far, must be recognized as a highly complicated composition whose central theme has several counterpoints. What is the central theme? Ostensibly it is the people's preparation for nationhood. Yet, as in all Bhattacharya's books, though this historic event is present, is felt, is to some degree motivational, it is really peripheral to the central action. What is central, it seems to me, is human character—essentially good, sound, compassionate. And it is on this character that the new nation is being founded. The ultimate test of nationhood will be the moral fibre of villagers such as these—impoverished, illiterate, superstitious perhaps, but hard-working, basically intelligent, and wise in tradition.

As Millen Brand, Bhattacharya's editor at Crown Publishers, points out, the "lure of easy solutions" has appeal for others as well as for the simple villagers of India: "Gold. A Goddess named Gold. The lure of easy solutions, of chimeric torment, of age-old greed. The division of Sonamitti is universal in its meanings. . . ."[5]

CHAPTER 7

Shadow from Ladakh

I *Historic Fact*

SOON after its publication in 1966 in the United States, *Shadow from Ladakh* received the coveted Sahitya Akademi Award from India's National Academy of Letters. Although this most recent work inspired the honor, it is evident from the citation (see Chapter 2) that the recognition was for Bhattacharya's entire distinguished career as a writer. There may be substance to the claim some critics have made that patriotic ardor contributed to the singling out of this particular book; however, judgment of its literary worth should not be thrown completely out of joint by such assumed motivation. It seems to this reader that in the novel a host of characters are developed with human reality, and that a multiplicity of events—both real and fictional—are presented and controlled with considerable mastery. In many respects the book exhibits a realization of the author's literary maturity.

Unfortunately, however, Bhattacharya obscures his skill as a novelist with an overt didacticism that he has avoided to a large extent in his other books, even though they may have been equally inspired by contemporary issues. Perhaps the chief trouble here is that the contemporary issue may seem to the average reader more political than social, in contrast to his earlier fiction. The "shadow" cast by the Ladakh problem darkens Bhattacharya's broader and more basic question that continues to face present-day India: How can the nation move its village-centered, rural masses forward into a technologically controlled world society without destroying the values of an ancient culture?

Although the concluding months of World War II are the historical setting for *So Many Hungers!* and *He Who Rides a Tiger*, as is impending nationhood for *A Goddess Named Gold* and *Music for Mohini*, in them the actual events of history are peripheral and only recurrently brought to mind—as they may very well have been for most of India's people. In them national and world circumstances are largely "unseen movers." In *Shadow*, however, the historical event moves almost to center stage and plays an insistent role. It was the nation's first threat from a great world power and, as such, probably had more direct impact on all the people—village peasants and city sophisticates—than had even World War II.

Before the fictional story is summarized, therefore, it would be desirable to deal first with the factual background.

Ladakh, high in the Himalayan mountains at the eastern edge of Kashmir, has for centuries been a point of friction between India and China. It is recorded that as early as the fifth century an Indian Rajah sent an embassy to the Chinese court over the matter of the suzerainty of the border at Ladakh. In 1914 Tibet and the British Government in India signed an agreement, defined by Sir Henry McMahon, by which a natural watershed line was accepted as a border demarcation between the two nations.

From the moment in October 1950 when Mao Tse-tung sent his forces into Tibet to "liberate" that autonomous nation from "capitalist reactionaries" and "return it to the motherland of China," the boundary agreement had been in jeopardy. Since China had not been involved in the negotiations a half-century earlier, she regarded them as having no bearing on Chinese territorial sovereignty.

In 1959 Chinese forces occupied a sector southeast of Ladakh. China claimed the territory as hers and built a road across it to facilitate communication with captive Tibet. Friction mounted over the years with no resolution through diplomatic channels until, in October 1962, China invaded the North-East Frontier Province (NEFP) between Bhutan and India.

Bhattacharya recapitulates the crux of the impasse through the thoughts of one of his main characters, Satyajit:

In slow stages [the Chinese] had surreptitiously annexed sixteen thousand square miles of territory that had been an integral part of India. Their claims were mounting still; they wanted fifty thousand square miles at the eastern end of the frontiers, south of the so-called McMahon Line, a demarcation that had simply formalized the traditional and customary boundary accepted over the ages. . . . That meant China's military might arrayed on the edge of the Indian plains. What would India's security be worth then? The hard-won freedom? (81)[1]

It is at this point that *Shadow from Ladakh* opens.

II   *The Crucible*

Deftly, in the opening pages of his novel, Bhattacharya indicates its intertwined themes: How can the India of the Gandhian heritage respond to and cope with the violent, destructive forces of this day? What happens to the doctrine of *ahimsa* (non-violence) in the face of a violence that threatens the lifestream of a nation? Can India maintain her spiritual integrity in a materialistically centered world order?

Returning from a World Peace Congress in Moscow is Suruchi, wife of Satyajit Sen, founder of Gandhigram, a village established on Gandhi's principles and way of life. During her attendance at the conference armed hostilities between China and India had erupted in Ladakh. The subject was assiduously avoided until a rabid verbal attack by a Chinese woman delegate, which came as a shock to Suruchi who had had faith in the decade's slogans of friendship between China and India.

With his novelist's skill Bhattacharya presages the essence of the dramatic tension ahead as Suruchi, on her long return trip, mulls over her Moscow experiences in relation to her simple, homespun life and India's impending struggle for survival. A sense of personal crisis is aroused when her daughter, Sumita, is not at the New Delhi airport to meet her but sends a note explaining that she remains at home because the existence of Gandhigram is threatened by the encroachment of neighboring Lohapur, where the steel mill is thrown into a frenzy of productivity by the trouble in Ladakh.

Satyajit is first viewed through Suruchi's mind as she recalls the path that led them to this point in their lives. We see him—as does she—as a man with intense devotion to Gandhi's high principles, but without the strength of character to help him live successfully in terms of those principles. Toward the close of the action, Suruchi assesses Satyajit's strength and weakness as he prepares for a massive peace march into Ladakh, imitative of Gandhi's Salt March to the shores of the Arabian Sea three decades earlier:

Here, in this supreme hour of his test, he would be prepared to exceed himself. He would go all the way that Gandhi would have gone. But Gandhi would have gone his way with absolute peace of mind; he was capable of accepting self-imposed death without the least ripple in his equanimity. Satyajit would be battling hard every hour, every minute; battling against the inner man, the common man whom he wanted to be uncommon. (338)

Although Satyajit is perhaps the least appealing of all the major characters, the author gives him credibility through depicting him as a complicated individual striving to live as single-mindedly as did "the Father of the Nation," whose ideals and career he emulates. He is wracked by a sense of his own inadequacy and by pangs of conscience as he falls short, again and again, of the impossible goal he has set for himself. He is at once a man of arrogant pride in presuming to succeed Gandhi as the spiritual leader of the nation and a man of pathetic humility as he struggles with his recognized weaknesses.

How would Gandhiji respond to the stresses of this year, of this day, Satyajit keeps asking himself, fourteen years after his *guru's* death. Within the limitations of his unimaginative mind, Satyajit brings forward only answers from the past. Completely eluding him is the living essence of Gandhi, by which he might envision the master's solutions to the stresses of a new time.

As opposition to Satyajit, Bhattacharya presents Bhashkar Roy, Chief Engineer of the Lohapur Steel Company, who is developing a veritable "Steeltown" next door to Gandhigram. The life, the goals, the methods of the men and their towns are seemingly diametrically opposed. Yet each man and each community is imbued to some degree with the attributes of the other.

Home after years of study and technical training in America, Roy has the energy and drive of the New World. He believes as much in his "mission" as Satyajit does in his.

Looking through Gandhi's eyes, Satyajit believes he has a vocation to oppose an inhuman system:

The fight was with the system that welded human beings to the machines. But that was not all. Mechanization, Gandhi had said, was inevitable when there was a dearth of labor. It became needless and an evil when there was a surplus of hands. The problem in India was not how to find leisure for the teeming millions in its villages, but how to utilize their idle hours. Gandhi was not against the kind of machine that helped an individual to add to his efficiency without turning him into its helpless slave. (29)

Satyajit, then, centers his village about the spinning wheel, the symbol of the "machine that helps the individual." Bhashkar, on the other hand, with all the self-assurance of one whose time has come, tells Satyajit:

"Oversimplification!" Steel means economic progress. Machine tools, tractors, big industrial plants, locomotives. Steel to fight poverty and hunger. But steel has gained a second meaning. It stands for our country's freedom. That is an inescapable fact, not to be changed by wishful thinking. Development plus defense—a compulsion of our current history." (30)

(Echoes of Prime Minister Nehru's exclamation on the dedication of the great Bhakra Dam, highest in the world: "*Here* is *my* temple!")

As China and India are opposed in ideology and life force at the mountainous borders of Ladakh, so Satyajit Sen and Bhashkar Roy are opposed in the meadows of Bengal. For these men, as for India, this is the test by fire of their ideals and their lives.

III *Backgrounds*

I have referred to Satyajit's purpose of renewing in his life the life of Gandhi and designing Gandhigram along the lines of Gandhi's prototypical village, and the difficulty the disciple has in measuring up to the master. This may be an oversimplification of Satyajit's problem, however. For Bhattacharya challenges Satyajit with a demanding double standard.

In Gandhigram Satyajit has attempted to achieve the ideal of community life he sees as the outgrowth of the combined teachings of the philosopher-poet Rabindranath Tagore and the diplomat-saint Mohandas Gandhi. These two towering souls of the culture of India were very different, not so much in the goals toward which they strove as in the means to be used in reaching those goals. Both were dedicated to the brotherhood of humankind. Both were imbued with reverence for India's heritage and with faith in her future. Both sought national independence through nonviolent means. Each respected and loved the other. Yet their inner natures and approaches to life were very different. They openly disagreed on many

crucial occasions. In his *Gandhi: The Writer*, Bhattacharya quotes
Prime Minister Nehru as follows:

No two persons could be so different from each other in their make-up or
temperaments. Tagore, the aristocratic artist, represented essentially the
cultural tradition of India, the tradition of accepting life in the fullness
thereof. . . . Gandhi, more a man of the people, almost the embodiment of
the Indian peasant, represented the other ancient tradition of India, that
of renunciation and asceticism. . . . Both, in their different ways, had a
world outlook, and both were at the same time wholly Indian. They seemed
to represent different but harmonious aspects of India and to complement
one another.[2]

In many of the challenges that face Satyajit, Bhattacharya represents him as responding ambiguously or contradictorily, almost
schizophrenically. In a greater, more noble character the genius of
these two might have fused and, reincarnated as one, might have
come forward to lead India into a new age. Satyajit is—as most
of us—too humanly limited, too spiritually frail to receive so awe-
some a rebirth. The subtlety—the very "Indianness"—of this characterization, it seems to me, is what one Western critic missed when
she charged the author with not having "legitimized" Satyajit's
character.

It was at Tagore's international, inter-caste school, Santiniketan,
that Satyajit and Suruchi had met and had married across caste
lines. It was there they shared the early happy years of married
life. What Bhattacharya has to say about the attractions of Santiniketan for the young Satyajit might almost be a page from the
author's early diary:

There could hardly be a more attractive setting. Santiniketan was away
from the distractions of cities. It was a land of red earth and fierce gales,
and a tiny streamlet passed meandering not far from the campus edge. There
were groves of fruit trees, and sweet-scented shrubs and flowering creepers
broke the sternness of the scene. Classes were held in tree shade, the boys
and girls seated on their own reed mats, and the teacher on a foot-high
pedestal. It was not rare for a class to stop when a songbird started warbling
in the branches overhead; the pupils would get more from that voice than
from the teacher.
Santiniketan was meant to be home and temple in one. But there was also
a real temple, one of glass, open on all sides to the flooding sunlight. It was
the school chapel, without altar or image. Here the poet or one of the teachers

gave a weekly discourse. No dogmatic teaching. The poet believed in a world religion—he called it the Religion of Man. (14–15)

As a young undergraduate, Bhattacharya had spent enchanted summers at Santiniketan. The beauty of the place and of its guardian spirit is still obviously a part of his present life. His fictional character, Satyajit, left Santiniketan and Tagore to follow in the footsteps of Gandhi. On his own return from study in England, Bhattacharya reluctantly refused the poet's invitation that he join the teaching staff, realizing he would, as he has said, "continue merely to be dazzled by him and would write in his mode and under his influence." He wanted to develop his own writing mastery, his own style.

From the enchantment of Santiniketan, its beauty and its international atmosphere, Satyajit traumatically uproots his family to accept the call of Gandhi to join his life of simple austerity in Sevagram.

A week afterward, they set out with only a few of their belongings—all the rest had to be discarded. The mud house assigned to you at Sevagram would need no modern furnishings; you sat on a floormat, slept on a string cot. Your clothes would be woven out of yarn produced on a spinning wheel, preferably your own. Kitchen gadgets were out of place—the food had to be the simplest peasant's fare. Money itself was a needless burden. So were several of your thought patterns, and you dropped them in the course of your long journey by train; you made your mind a clean slate before you entered the village, covering the eight miles of roadway from Wardah station by a one-horse tandem. . . .

. . . A fact to note was that, before entering the new village, Satyajit Sen discarded his surname denoting caste affiliation. As simply Satyajit he would be casteless. (20)

A few years after taking up their new life, while Suruchi is still a young woman in her twenties, Satyajit embraces *bramacharya*, "complete chastity of body and even of thought." His efforts to hold to this demanding ideal wrack husband and wife in soul and body. Each defection is to Suruchi a moment of delight captured from an innocently passionate past; to Satyajit, it is a soul-wrenching defection to carnal weakness.

It is against these backgrounds that Satyajit, soon after Gandhiji's assassination, founded Gandhigram where all inhabitants would live in accordance with the teachings of the martyr. Most faithful of the followers is his daughter, twenty-year-old Sumita, who regards Satyajit as truly the saint he aspires to be. Barefoot, free of jewels and bangles, dressed in a simple white sari of hand-loomed *khadi*, Sumita's beauty glows with youth and spiritual devotion.

IV *Conflict*

The air is weighted with the conflict that has erupted at the border of Ladakh. For Satyajit, however, of more immediate concern is the conflict at the border of Gandhigram and Lohapur, where the steel mill seeks room for the expansion that is now a part of the nation's struggle for survival. It is this conflict that is also one of the author's chief concerns.

The most frequent adverse criticism of *Shadow from Ladakh* is that it is too politically oriented. To this Bhattacharya replies that Chinese aggression is not the story. Actually the story is what happens because of that aggression. All the forces that affect Gandhigram and Lohapur become more immediate and more intense; they must be tackled immediately. The Ladakh emergency serves as a sort of catalyst. The reaction of the protagonists is quickened. Central is the conflict between two ways of life, and history is used just to make the forces come together quickly.[3]

In response to the national crisis, "Americanized" Bhashkar Roy drives himself and his employees without mercy. The steel mill must be expanded at once. The first, logical step is acquisition of the level meadow land lying between village and town. Next, probably inevitably, will be Gandhigram itself, which Bhashkar sees not only as a desirable land area but as an ideological opposition that hinders his progress. Bhashkar and Satyajit seek the same goals—eradication of poverty and preservation of the nation's freedom. But how different the means toward those goals! In his first confrontation with Satyajit and Sumita, Bhashkar Roy impatiently puts aside their points of view:

. . . Steel means economic progress. Machine tools, tractors, big industrial plants, locomotives. Steel to fight poverty and hunger. But steel has gained a second meaning. It stands for our country's freedom. That is an inescapable fact, not to be changed by wishful thinking. Development plus defense—a compulsion of our current history. To meet the demands is far from easy. We have no choice, though. . . . We have to get steel, more and more, at any price. The pace of production must quicken. (30–31)

To this Sumita replies: "Any price? What about human obliga-
tions?" And Bhashkar: "Ends justify means."

Satyajit shook his head. "You can never attain good through evil. That
was the essence of all that Gandhi-ji had to say." (32)

How can the Bhashkar Roy philosophy ever be accommodated
to the Gandhian philosophy by which Satyajit and his village live?

The village with its two hundred mud houses, seeking to build a set of
values. Values to be lived, to be expressed in terms of deed. Complete equal-
ity, unreserved fraternity. Limitless non-violence, as much in thought as in
action. Slogans glibly voiced everywhere; in Gandhigram they had to be
real. The Gandhian village was not its mud walls alone. It was spirit. The
spirit of man striving to transcend the physical. (49)

Although the international conflagration may not be the core
of the novel's action, Bhattacharya maintains it is necessary for
the dramatic purposes of his story. He once wrote:

I saw somewhere a comment that *Shadow* did not have to be set during the
Chinese attack. That is a wrong comment. The time frame I selected was a
technical need. The conflict between Gandhigram and Steeltown could
attain urgency, intensity, edge . . . only in a crisis like the one depicted.[4]

This insistence on the pertinence of the border confrontation,
however, serves mainly to emphasize that the real essence of the
conflict is not the Sino-Indian border war, nor the concrete physical
confrontation brought by the expansion of Steeltown. The opposition is between two ways of life, which the author makes clear
throughout the book. As the Himalayan conflict intensifies and the
demands for supplies increase, the engineer is convinced that Steeltown must "fight to annex Gandhigram. To annex, not a village,
but an entire way of life. There couldn't be two Indias, back to back,
gazing at opposite horizons, ready to march off and get further
and further apart." (59)

Which course—that of Satyajit or that of Bhashkar Roy—will
bring together the two personalities of India to see and march as
one into the future? Can it, indeed, be either, or must it be both
reaching some sort of working accord?

It is typical of the Bhattacharya life view that his characters seek an amalgamation. One point of view does not eventually defeat and obliterate the other. This is also typical, it seems to me, of the Asian mind. As the *yin* (female, dark, negative) has within it an essence of *yang* (male, light, affirmative), so has the *yang* an essence of *yin*. Only in a balance of these two life forces can physical and spiritual health be realized. The great holy scripture of Hinduism, the *Bhagavad Gita*, reconciles action with knowledge and devotion, its activism being "tinged with an element of renunciation."[5]

But, more directly, perhaps, there was Tagore's lifelong influence on Bhattacharya. Through the thoughts of Suruchi, Tagore's belief in the possibility of meeting on a common ground is given:

That was Tagore's firm belief. Integration—that was the poet's lifelong quest: integration of the simple and the sophisticated; the ancient and the modern; city and village; East and West.

"Keep this in mind, Sumita," [admonishes Suruchi]. "The poet didn't believe, as many do, that uniformity has to be the bedrock basis of unity." (215)

This sort of resolution of opposites is regarded as a weakness by some Western reviewers of *Shadow*, one of whom finds the "final accommodation of one world to the other" to be "quite disappointing" after all the to-do over the conflict.[6] Another sees it as "fudging and punch-pulling."[7]

Personally, I consider it the only resolution consonant with the author's heritage and guiding philosophy.

V *Humor and Satire*

Shadow from Ladakh is probably Bhattacharya's weightiest and most serious work (with the possible exception of *So Many Hungers!*): yet it is lightened by humorous scenes and characters.

In the village, Great-Uncle is the recipient of considerable reverence because of his advanced age, but he is also the source of much amusement. Most deeply rooted in the past, the only remaining illiterate within these Gandhian mud walls, Great-Uncle nevertheless has closer ties with the confusing modern world of technology than do any of his neighbors. His grandson has gone to work in the steelmill and his glowing accounts of life in the "big town" threaten the roots of Gandhigram. Scenes such as this one ring

with the authenticity of the author's keen observation and sym-
pathetic understanding of village ways:

> [Sumita] went to the door. What could have brought Great-Uncle to the
> schoolhouse?
> He flaunted a yellow envelope in his hand. "Letter from that pig of a grand-
> son who's gone to Lohapur. The housefolk all away on errands—who will
> read it out to me?" A note of hesitation came to his voice. "You . . . ?" . . .
> "Of course, Great-Uncle."
> "Private letter, this. For my hearing only. . . . Not for your hearing. First
> clap your forefingers to your ears—hard—so that no word can get in. Hold
> the fingers pressed hard." . . .
> Her hands went up, obeying, to her ears.
> "What now? The letter? Have I three hands, Great-Uncle?"
> "I will hold each sheet before your face. So . . . !" He peered, making
> sure her ears were closed, then gestured to her to proceed. (75)

But the most broadly humorous (and the term is used advisedly!)
is Mrs. Sarojini Mehra, personal secretary (P.S.) to the Chief
Engineer (C.E.), Bhashkar Roy. The Lohapur Steel Mill may produce the parts for motor-driven vehicles, but the C.E.'s P.S. gets
about town on her bicycle "her ample buttocks spilling over the
spring seat." "As she pushed the pedals her plump thighs worked
like steam-driven propellers, and beads of sweat broke out on her
nose and upper lip." (95)
Mrs. Mehra brings the same remorseless energy to her manipulation of the lives of others as she does to her machine. A combination
of excessive efficiency and honest concern for the welfare of her asso-
ciates leads her to intervene constantly in their affairs. Since her
devotion to the C.E. is almost equal to that for her self-effacing
husband, it is Bhashkar who must suffer through most of her
ministrations. Generally he submits, following the course of least
resistance.
Wayward threads through the somber weave of much of the
story come from the shuttle set in motion by Mrs. Mehra when
she places a marriage ad for the bachelor C.E., unbeknown to him,
presenting him simultaneously with both replies and advertising
bill. The society matrons of the swank Lohapur Club are activated
when they deduce that only Bhashkar Roy could be the advertise-
ment's "handsome high-salaried Company executive (33). America
returned, with ultramodern outlook" who seeks a helpmate to

share his twelve-room "mansion." (93) Special occasions are devised
to bring the C.E. to his inevitable destiny as daughters are prepared
for the joyous sacrifice. In the frequent defections of the groom-
to-be, Mrs. Mehra enjoys the festivities in his stead. She who has
been scorned and socially *de trop*, now finds herself the "catch" of
the season.

Satire, sweetened by humor, sparks all the characters and scenes
having to do with the Lohapur Club. Since the Club's mores, as
well as its building, are the heritage from British Colonial society,
we recognize the author's double-edged barb.

A climactic satirical scene brings together the diverse elements
of the group's social snobbery, the mothers' schemes to ensnare
Bhashkar, and the government's call for war funds and warm
clothing for India's troops suffering in mountain temperatures. A
knitting contest pits the two top social leaders in a do-or-die battle
for supremacy, and a dramatic gift of personal jewelry is designed
to impress the C.E. with a daughter's beauty of body and spirit.
Both devices spell disaster rather than triumph for the contenders.

In another area of interpersonal relationships Mrs. Mehra meets
with more success. Bhattacharya dramatizes, on the limited stage
of Lohapur, a widespread social tension that accompanied the
Ladakh incident: popular uprisings against Chinese nationals resi-
dent in India. In Lohapur the shoemaker, Ah To, being the only
Chinese, takes the full brunt of social and government disfavor.
When his five daughters are persecuted by their schoolmates and
when Ah To is taken into "protective custody," Mrs. Mehra goes
into action. She moves the children into Bhashkar Roy's "mansion,"
informing him after the fact. Rupa, a beautiful half-American girl
who is an assistant executive at the mill, is then called in as their
private tutor. The story of Bhashkar's increasing emotional involvement with the children and with Rupa is an appealing one.
Out of unlikely material a family is formed. The amity in this
household reinforces in basic human terms the Prime Minister's
insistence that hatred of the Chinese people should not be a by-
product of the war. The author quotes a warning from Nehru:

"I would like to stress that I do not want that aspect of the cold war or hot
war which leads to hatred of a whole people. I hope no such emotion will
rise in our country. We have nothing against the Chinese people. We must
not transfer our anger and bitterness at what has been done by the Chinese
Government to the Chinese people."

Bhashkar let his glance rest fondly on the alien inmates of his household, and the idea struck him that the five Chinese girls were at war, too! Slender and small, they were fighting the battle of humanity, which their vast, powerful country had already lost. Their victory over a minute area of the spirit had to make up for all the inner poverty that the leaders of their ancient race were showing today. (256–57)

VI   *Opposing Forces*

Bhashkar's response to the Ladakh emergency is wholly in terms of energetic, almost frenetic, action. Every barrier to the fullest possible production of steel must be crushed. If Gandhigram is an obstacle, quite logically it must go.

Bhashkar, however, finds himself caught in opposing forces both without and within. Twelve years in the United States did not, after all, make a crude industrialist of him. If it had, he could have moved ruthlessly against Gandhigram, and, in the personal realm, the ultramodern Westernized Rupa would have conquered his heart with no difficulty. But, with each passing day, his innate Indianness reasserts itself with increasing strength. No one recognizes this better than Rupa herself. During one of their last conversations, she says to Bhashkar:

"The truth is that America as a whole has meant nothing to you. You brought back the industrial know-how. Not the know-how of life! This is the case with every Indian. He goes West and becomes a new person. He returns home and at once he is a complete Indian. . . . Technical knowledge is your only link with the West." (317)

The reawakening of his cultural awareness and his growing respect for Suruchi and love for Sumita begin to weaken Bhashkar's assault against the neighboring village.

Satyajit responds to the national challenge in Gandhian terms. He will lead a "Peace March" into the embattled area. With five from Gandhigram itself—one being Sumita—he will inspire a mass response that will take hundreds, or even thousands, to the very borders of China. Surely the Chinese leaders will recognize the force of the nonviolent demonstration, will halt their aggression, and once more both sides of the border will echo to the once-popular cries of *Chinee-Hindi, bhai, bhai*! ("Chinese-Indians, brothers, brothers!") which had rung through city streets and village marketplaces almost a decade ago.

When China unexpectedly withdraws her troops across the Bhutan border and a ceasefire is declared, Satyajit's march is cancelled—fortunately, for it had elicited little response. The battle lines remain drawn at home, however, and Satyajit now concentrates on saving his village. His weapon will be another forged in the fire of Gandhi's spirit—a fast unto death, unless the Government unconditionally refuses the steel company's request that Gandhigram be ceded to it for its expansion.

That these opposing forces, represented by Bhashkar and Satyajit, cannot remain unalterably opposed is foreshadowed from the very beginning of the novel. The reader has been given the basic ingredients with which to realize what the outcome will be. There must inevitably be a resolution of opposites, an accommodation to differing points of view. Not only is this the author's philosophy, as has been said, but it is basically Indian. Through character delineation and interaction and through expert use of symbols, Bhattacharya clears the way for the final scenes in which Gandhigram and Steeltown will join forces in affirmation of the unique elements each brings to a modern India.

Bhashkar, the man of steel, turns to the spinning wheel for the peace and spiritual composure his life requires. Symbolically, it is his favorite Chinese "daughter," Erh-ku, who has brought the wheel home from Gandhigram and who teaches him to use it.

Bhashkar [now] devoted a half hour every day to the wheel. Would it simply be a mechanical gesture? Or would he gain from that gesture some element of the spirituality with which the simple wooden implement was vested? (331)

Satyajit's "fast unto death" arouses the practical-minded steel workers as well as his own people. They join the villagers in vigils around the clock.

It was in this curious circumstance that one of Bhashkar's dreams was fulfilled: Steeltown began to move toward Gandhigram! Scores of millhands, both men and women, stood anxious-eyed near Satyajit's house, waiting for the latest news on his health. Silent, or else speaking in low tones to the village-folk who crowded up to them. There could be no easier intermingling. Satyajit filled the thoughts of all. . . . When the visitors had crossed the threshhold of the homes, all barriers between city and village were gone. The slogan of brotherhood, enriched with emotional content, became real. . . . The divisions were gone. (352)

But the move is not one of the absorption of one neighbor by the other, of the ancient cultural and spiritual traditions by the crass materialism of a new age. It is an intermixture of the two. When the workers strike in behalf of Satyajit's cause, Bhashkar and the government look in other directions for the mill's expansion and the impasse is resolved. Each community will contribute value and strength to the other. In this sort of cooperative accord resides India's only hope for the future.

As has been said, Bhattacharya utilizes symbols with considerable dexterity in all his novels. The spinning wheel, which the people of Gandhigram use daily, representing both the traditions of India and the spirit of Gandhi. Rupa, half-American, half-Indian, a living representation of the uneasy adjustment of two sets of values within one body, yet the hope for the future. Sumita ("wisdom"), calm, with a deep strength rooted in ancient traditions, being awakened now to the attractions and repulsions of a disturbing new way of life. Bhashkar, representative of the thousands of young men and women who return home from years abroad to find themselves challenged by readjustment to ancient ways, feeling the tightening bonds he had supposed were broken. The five little Chinese girls demonstrating the power of unspoiled trust and love to overcome the barriers of misunderstanding, even hate.

If we recognize symbolism in the characters, somewhat as proposed above, we would be justified in concluding that Bhattacharya himself was not too sure in which direction India should (or would) go at the time of his writing *Shadow from Ladakh*. Will the future be increasingly dominated by Western values and skills or will it work toward what might be called an "enlightened traditionalism"? Bhattacharya has said that, at the outset, he planned on bringing Bhashkar and Rupa together. But, in the end, Sumita wins his heart. In an interview with *Mahfil*[8] Bhattacharya was asked whether he sees any resolution of India's dilemma in being caught in a "conflict between traditional and modern values," and why is Rupa moved out of the picture "rather unhappily"? Bhattacharya replied:

A novelist does not *state*—he simply dramatizes. But I think it is evident in the final scene in *Shadow from Ladakh* that co-existence is the answer.

As for Rupa, it was no fault of hers (not, that is, of the makings in her) that Bhashkar falls in love with Sumita. Characters have a volition of their own. . . . They challenge the intention of their creator as they give shape and meaning to their own lives. I had originally planned that Bhashkar would marry Rupa—the two belong to the same world, while Sumita inhabited another. But I was thwarted!

Mahfil: Bhashkar and Satyajit are also blends of East and West, modernity and tradition, though with different proportions of these qualities in the two; Bhashkar, with an abundance of Westernism and Satyajit, with an abundance of Indianism. What is the significance of giving Satyajit the final victory with his death fast?

DR. BHATTARCHARYA: Is it correct to say that Satyajit gets the ultimate victory? The victory, I think, is shared by the two opponents. After all, Satyajit loses his daughter for whom he had wanted a different kind of destiny and fulfillment. As for Bhashkar, he accepts some of the values for which Gandhigram stands as a symbol. Modern industrialism with its spiritual corrosion redeems itself with a new purity of purpose, a sense of complete dedication.

VII *Divided Opinion*

Bhattacharya himself calls *Shadow from Ladakh* his favorite novel. In his *Mahfil* interview he said: "I loved every minute of the writing, which did not involve the slightest strain." He made much the same remark to me, though he added he was "more emotionally involved" with *So Many Hungers!*, his first novel.

Of all Bhattacharya's writing this novel has elicited the most sharply divided critical opinions. The Sino-India conflict and its obtrusion (or non-obtrusion) into the story line seem to be the main subjects of disagreement. The critic's reaction may depend to some extent upon his relationship—geographical or ideological—to the crisis events. The book has enjoyed a natural popularity at home, where it has been translated into Hindi, Marathi, and Bengali. Although the Dutch version has done well, as of this writing no Russian translation had yet appeared.

It is interesting to juxtapose some of the opposed points of view.

Humayun Kabir, at the time India's Minister of Education, found didacticism successfully avoided:

I have read *Shadow from Ladakh* with great interest and enjoyed the skill with which Bhabani Bhattarcharya has presented some problems of modern India through the clash of personalities. The struggle between old values and new is a perennial human problem, and has become particularly keen in India. The danger is that such studies may become didactic, but Bhabani Bhattacharya is first and foremost an artist and has avoided the danger successfully. With a few deft touches, he has brought to life the Gandhian hero and his modern antagonist. The other characters also are vivid and yet in some ways, the character of Suruchi is the most vital though she appears but rarely.[9]

Patricia L. Sharpe,[10] on the other hand, sees *Shadow from Ladakh* as not much more than patriotic propaganda that "probably made literary officialdom feel very good." She condemns Bhattacharya for his failure to offer a neat solution to the complex problem presented in *Shadow from Ladakh* (a problem of human and political involvements that may take a generation to resolve) at the same time as she illogically accuses him of habitually turning to "clever manipulative device" to resolve the dilemmas his characters confront.

Thomas Lask, writing in *The New York Times*, finds a satisfying unity in the diverse elements brought together in *Shadow from Ladakh*. Probably he puts his finger on the sore spot that so distresses Ms. Sharpe when he surmises that "the conclusion the book provides will . . . surprise Westerners more than Mr. Bhattacharya's own people." One suspects that Ms. Sharpe has not entered sufficiently into the world of the characters to appreciate their response to the opposing forces in which they are embroiled. Acknowledging that the novel is "guided by ideas rather than by character," Lask goes on to conclude that the author "can put these ideas into the mouths of his people without making them sound stilted or rhetorical" and he finds them "worth meeting."

Finally—whereas *India Briefing*, a publication of The Asia Society, terms *Shadow from Ladakh* "something more than mere documentary fiction" and praises the author for bringing history "to life through its impact on human beings," reviewer Sarah Ensley Brandel,[11] finds the novel "only mildly interesting." Like Ms. Sharpe she, too, faults Bhattacharya for investigating "several possibilities for resolving the conflict" symbolized by Gandhigram and Steeltown without attempting "a penetrating analysis of the psychological tensions of living in these conflicting worlds" or finding the secret solution in his "crystal ball."

The individual reader is best left to his own critical response, it would seem, with the admonition that he make every possible effort to leave his own cultural bias before entering the world of Satyajit, Suruchi and Sumita—or, even, for that matter, the Western-influenced world of Bhashkar Roy and Rupa.

CHAPTER 8

Essayist and Teller of Tales

A LTHOUGH Bhattacharya is regarded by himself and his readers chiefly as a novelist, he has written many essays and is a prolific short-story writer. Unfortunately, it is impossible to assess these facets of his career with any sense of adequacy, for apparently he has kept no careful record of his shorter pieces. Essays and stories have been written, published in various journals, payment received, copies kept or not kept, and that has been the end of it for their creator. A fair sense of the story output may be got, however, from the impressive listing of translations into German which have been done by Erica Kalmer (see Bibliography), who has served as Bhattacharya's literary agent in placing the German language versions of his work.

I Realism and Cultural "Interplay"

Three main streams of social and literary philosophy run throughout most of Bhattacharya's articles, essays, and talks—(1) the social purposes of literature, (2) the development of bridges of understanding between cultures, especially East and West, and (3) English as a medium of international communication.

In "Literature and Social Reality"[1] Bhattacharya asserts that many Indian writers have equated esthetic refinement with detachment from the living reality in which their writing should be rooted. In their eagerness to avoid charges of "tendentiousness" they too often yield to escapism or sentimentality. Like Tolstoy, Gandhi, and Rolland before him, Bhattacharya impatiently rejects the ready philosophy of "art for art's sake." Such a view he finds "as queer . . . as, say, science for the sake of science." Furthermore, "with the world shrunken in size and under more and more pressure to be monolithic, as it were, from forces that seem to have laws of their own, how could one set of ideas, one class of human endeavor be insulated from another? How could values in art help getting involved in the values of human living?"

The central core of Bhattacharya's argument is his fundamental, compelling belief that the creative writer can no more write in a vacuum than any one of us can live dissociated from society. And how can the creative writer be "non-partisan," as so many lay claim to being? "The creative writer's final business," Bhattacharya asserts, "is to reveal the truth. . . . And how could the truth help being partisan?"

To scholars who are studying Bhattacharya's genius in revealing the female psyche there is special interest in the way in which he opens this discussion of social reality by referring to the contemporary analyses that find in the fairy tales of early times "a labyrinth of motives, a complex of reactions." He writes (back in 1955, we note):

So it is that Cinderella is not honestly two-dimensional, an accepted myth or romance, as of old. She is a real person stumbling through life under the propulsion of her Unconscious. *What is more pathetic, and sometimes abhorrent, is that she has to act as a "woman" must.* The so-called romantic writer of today seems to woo actuality by depicting in detail and with sharp photographic accuracy the sex convolutions of his Cinderella and his Prince, thus giving them roots, apparently, in the common earth of life and time. [Italics mine.]

Three later essays dwell on the growing need for a world community, an interchange and accommodation among the various human cultures, but especially between Asia and the West.

"A Bridge between the Peoples"[2] opens with the assertions "There is a vast lot of Europe in today's Asia. There is a vast lot of Asia in today's Europe." and then goes on to argue that uniformity, however, "is not an essential ingredient of unity."

Bhattacharya's metaphoric bridge is presented as a two-way thoroughfare, "as genuine a link as a structure of steel and concrete," carrying "a hundred diversities—diversities of tradition, form, experience, revolt, reconstruction." He rejects the concept of "cultural exchange," frequently lauded as the most effective international panacea, contending that "we do not actually part with some of our culture and take something of another culture in return. . . . We give and yet retain everything and in addition we make an acquisition." He prefers the idea of an "interplay" of cultures based on the mutual acceptance of "the idea that no country is culturally superior to others."

The discussion of the interplay of cultures concludes with an assertion of the continuing ties between England and India established largely in an "inner kinship" developed through a shared literary heritage.

For well over a century, we in India have been intensely absorbed in the spirit of English literature. While we have learnt highly developed techniques, we have attained something else—a compassionate understanding of the life reflected in that literature. We fought our battles of freedom against the British rulers of the country, but we seldom lost our deeper links with the British mind. . . . The inexorable fact stands that we want no severance of our mind's relationship with the people of Britain, a relationship that their literature has fostered. English literature continues to be a solid bridge between India and the United Kingdom.

Significantly, the essay ends with a defense of the Indian author who chooses to use English as his medium. He attacks as "shallow and unwarranted" the "growing tendency in India to regard writers in [English] as a special caste or sect insulated from others." He counters such attacks by the assertion that "Indian writers in English have their roots as deeply imbedded in the earth of their people's life as all the others." Certainly, Bhattacharya's own writing adds substance to his claim.

Similar lines of reasoning run through an unpublished paper[3] on the general theme "After Vietnam, What?" There Bhattacharya fuses his scholarly background as historian and social scientist with the expressive power of the creative writer. Opening with a call to "move forward from the dark realities of yesterday and the long-drawn twilight of today into the potentialities of tomorrow," the writer envisions a "humanization" of a ravaged people. "Americanization, Vietnamization, humanization—thus the wheel turns a full circle."

The Indian author, reading his paper before a largely American gathering, has the courage to enunciate a conviction he realizes is generally unpopular at the time—his belief in "American idealism." He sees "light prevailing over darkness" as the world moves into the future. He sees Americans and Asians working as "equal partners in a vast enterprise" to reestablish human values, not only

in Vietnam, but throughout the world. In equal partnership West
and East will no longer be held "artificially apart" but they together
will create a destiny that will be "something other than the doom
of transformation into handsful of radio-active ash!"

Peripheral to the main thesis in this paper, but an important
element in Bhattacharya's personal philosophy, is his rebuttal of a
popular idea in India that her culture must remain unaffected by
alien ways:

> Puerile arguments had been used even by Indian educationists who must
> have known better that close contact with alien cultures would make Indians
> lose their own identity. It was conveniently forgotten that the very concept
> of Indian nationalism was born in the universities of Britain. Most of our
> top-ranking national leaders had their education in those universities. Far
> from losing their identity, they launched the powerful struggle that brought
> the country complete independence from alien rule.

II   A Return to Sources

In "The Nature of Wisdom," written on request of Abbott
Universal Ltd. for the first issue of its international journal of
science, culture, and the arts,[4] Bhattacharya returns to a major
source of Indian wisdom, the *Bhagavad Gita*, to throw light on a
path of action for the contemporary world. Even here, however,
as he re-explores a basically Hindu response to life, he rejects the
assumption of an exclusive superiority in Hindu roots of wisdom.
He states at the outset:

> It is my purpose here to present certain facets of the Hindu view which seem
> to me attractive in the context of the present day. Not that I claim for this
> view any sanctity or even a semblance of superiority. It is simply one path
> of life among many others. . . .

Turning to the life examples of the Vedic sage Yagnavalkya and
his wife Maitreyi and to the philosophy of the *Bhagavad Gita*, Bhattacharya dwells on the teaching that stresses union of thought with
action. "Ancient Indian thought orientated this genre of action with
the nature of wisdom," he writes. Concerned solely with the *Gita's*
preoccupation with the inevitability of action, he is not interested
here in an exploration of its other teachings:

The *Gita's* socio-ethical values do not concern me here—they have many points of contact with what is available in other major scriptural works. . . . What gives the *Gita* its own individuality is its strong insistence on the establishment of a dynamic equilibrium in the art of living. That equilibrium is essential in both intra-personal and inter-personal relationships, and is the way of self-fulfilment.

Even here, where Bhattacharya focuses on one of India's major religio-social contributions to world culture—the union of wisdom and selfless action—he eschews the temptation to cultural chauvinism. In the course of the brief essay he even takes pains to point out that the saintly Mahatma Gandhi, "whose entire life-work was based on what he believed to be the fundamental message of the *Gita*," first came to the great classic of Hinduism by way of Sir Edwin Arnold's masterly English translation.

In "Tagore as a Novelist"[5] Bhattacharya returns to another rich source of Indian life and thought. As in his biography of Gandhi, he here deals with only one aspect of a life that for three-quarters of a century was crowded with creative achievement.[6]

The opening paragraphs of the essay on Tagore have special interest, for they reveal as much about Bhattacharya's views of the writer's craft as they do about Tagore. Bhattacharya begins his discussion of Tagore, the novelist, with a statement of his own concepts of the differing roles of poet and novelist:

It will perhaps be a truism to say that the creative roles of the poet and the novelist are not interchangeable. While both, at their best, are intensely concerned with the basic values of life, they are apart in spirit and in discipline. It is no wonder that seldom in world literature has a novelist written great poetry; and it is hard to conceive that any poet could ever create a *War and Peace*. Rabindranath Tagore, one of the greatest poets of all time, wrote several novels, but this work as a whole may not claim to have attained the stature of his best poetry. Yet the superb richness that is strewn in almost reckless profusion in the great volume of his verses is also to be found in his short stories. That is understandable. There is a kinship between the verse and the short story as literary forms. The short story was intrinsically suited to Tagore's temperament and it could carry the strongest echoes of his essentially poetic genius.

Bhattacharya's own writing might also be measured by the standards he sets down here. Later in this chapter, I express my personal view that the short-story form is not the best vehicle for

Bhattacharya's thought. He uses more effectively the broader view and the more leisurely pace of the novel. While Tagore is first and foremost poet, Bhattacharya is first and foremost novelist. The confinements of the brief story, to which the poet may submit with relative ease, are unnaturally restrictive for the novelist.

To return to Tagore—although Bhattacharya judges that Tagore's novels fall short of the excellence of his poetry and stories, he finds it nevertheless true that "even in the field of longer fiction Tagore's contribution to Bengali literature is unique and still unequaled." He places Tagore among the "pioneers" of Bengali novelists and hails him especially for setting up "a new literary genre in Bengal, the realistic novel, in which story values are based . . . on characterization and psychological content." *Chokher Bali*, 1902 (translated into English as *Binodini*) he claims as "the earliest work of its kind [the realistic novel] in any Indian language." *Gora*, 1909, he calls "the greatest of all his novels . . . contemporary and yet timeless."

III   *Critics Criticized*

In "Hollow Arbiters of the Writer's Destiny"[7] Bhattacharya has written one of his few acerbic pieces. His observations on the often unwarranted power of literary critics to make or break creative writers are based on considerable reading of reviews in India and abroad, on bitter personal experience as an author subject to arbitrary treatment, and on his own brief career as an editor. Although he touches on journalistic practices abroad, his chief concern is with the way in which books are reviewed in India's newspapers and literary journals. Too frequently, he contends, the commentator is a frustrated writer who is more concerned with demonstrating his own brilliance and writer's art than in evaluating the work he has set out to assess. He comes at this point head-on in the opening sentences of his essay:

It has been stated, maybe somewhat sweepingly, that would-be authors (creative ones in particular), when they fail to place their book-manuscripts with publishers, turn their frustration into the stuff of cynical zest and record stern critics of the work of their successful fellow-writers. This is even believed to be the real genesis of the art or craft of book reviews!

After speaking of the bitter experience of the young Keats, whose early verse was the subject of ridicule by "a third-rate scribe of the

Edinburgh Review," Bhattacharya goes on to relate the way in which his own first book was treated in a Bombay paper:

With a beating heart, I waited for the reviews to appear. The very first one, printed in a Bombay paper, was one of the most painful shocks in all my experience. Every word in its fifteen-or-so lines was dipped in venom. (It was an unsigned review.) One would not need a great deal of imagination to realize my tormented state of mind. (My first novel, remember, and one on which my future writing career was to be based.) I came to the dismal conclusion that I was not destined to be a creative writer.

Fortunately, the fate of *So Many Hungers!* and of Bhabani Bhattacharya as novelist did not rest solely on this first review. After the London edition of the novel appeared, enthusiastic evaluations were published there and in India.

In "Baseless Prejudice Against Indians Writing English" Bhattacharya tackles another "touchy" subject in an essay-length article written for *The Statesman* (August 1968). Here he deals with an issue referred to earlier that not only has affected his literary career but is a matter of almost visceral conviction. Soon after the achievement of independence there was a nationalist groundswell in affirmation of all things Indian and a rejection of "foreign importations" —even the English language, which was India's advantageous link with the world. Use of English was grudgingly endorsed for business and diplomatic purposes, but not for the creative writer. As Bhattacharya puts it in the opening sentences of his essay:

Nehru wrote in English, in English alone, and attracted no brickbats. Dr. Radhakrishnan as well, and several others of top literary calibre. The limp explanation goes that so long as you keep away from creative writing in English you will be free from attack.

He goes on to point out that no such prejudice hampered Indian authors in early periods "when India was tethered to British rule." This he finds ironic and a "freakish contradiction." As has been related earlier (Chapter 2), Bhattacharya made a deliberate decision during his student days in London to use English, rather than Bengali, as his linguistic medium. He reached his decision from his own predilection and with the advice of *Spectator* editor Francis Yeats-Brown and of the great Tagore himself. Yet, throughout his writing career he has been subjected to barbed—often virulent—

attack by some Indian critics for this choice. The rebuttal he gives here has the force of sound logic and basic conviction:

The grime of its imperialistic association washed away, the English language takes on for us a new visage: it is not the language of the United Kingdom alone: it has a rich, profuse fruit-bearing beyond the shores of its origin. Having gained this depth of view we do not have to be obsessed any more by our old emotional scars. But the hard fact is that the old scars throb in the manner of new wounds. The result is unfortunate.

He goes on to one of his favorite points—the need for building bridges of understanding between peoples—a conviction that runs throughout his life and work.

In an age when Indian nationalism stands fulfilled and may be expected to flow out and get lost in the swell of world-streams, the demand grows strident that language be used as an instrument of self-insulation, not of inter-communication and cohesion.

The most potent means of cohesion is creative literature, which makes a bridge between the peoples of the world. A many-spanned bridge reaching out over vast areas of space and of time as well, it is designed to carry a two-way traffic, outward and inward, regardless of volume and weight. That traffic eliminates distances far more effectively than even jet propulsion.

An accident of history (or whatever else it is) has ordained that English, admittedly a great international language, is to be our main transport vehicle on this two-way bridge.

From this thesis given in generalized terms, Bhattacharya goes on to relate his personal experience in attending a writer's conference, sponsored by the Government of India, in which he and South Indian novelist, R. K. Narayan, found themselves "two wrong men" in a group in which all others wrote in their regional languages.

"Is it possible to write creatively in a foreign tongue?" That was a typical question which drew from the participants the blunt answer that it was not. Take the instance of the novelist, they said. He could not reproduce Indian speech through English dialogue, nor could he render the subtle nuances of Indian thought, custom and character. Further, since the writers in English had perpetually in view a foreign audience with its known fancy for the exotic, the off-beat, they were not taken seriously by Western literary critics. Whatever reputation thay had earned was just ephemeral. They would find no place in the history of English literature, while every important writer in Hindi and Bengali and Tamil would have a cosy nook in their respective literary annals.

The debate led to a somewhat startling conclusion. Writers in English, it was stated, would do well to employ their linguistic ability in translating the best works in the regional languages and place them before a world audience. That way they could obtain the substance of satisfaction for which they quested in vain through their own original writing.

How familiar the arguments sound! I, too, have heard them enunciated with apparent sincerity at writers' conferences more widely representative of other tongues and cultures than the meeting of thirty Indian writers to which Bhattacharya refers here. The attack is invariably the same—indeed, identical to the attack that teachers and publishers of "the old school" make against the attempt to translate alien (especially non-Western) literatures into other languages. Bhattacharya rebuts this argument with force:

Undeniably, it is far more difficult to write creatively in a foreign language than in one's own. All the same, the principle has to be conceded and affirmed that a writer must have complete freedom to express himself in whatever language he likes, just as the selection of theme and the way of approach to the material must be entirely his own business. If creative writing is to be free from fetters, there can be no place for linguistic compulsions. Those who write in English can hardly be unaware of the technical problems they must solve. To render the atmosphere of one way of life in the literary idiom of another may easily be a heart-breaking effort. Many undertones of feeling if not thought, aptly conveyed in Indian words, are not fully transferable in alien linguistic equivalents. Above all, to place Indian realities before foreign readers with their near-total ignorance about the deeper springs of life in this country must call for a creative skill far higher than what a writer will normally need. If, in face of all these hurdles, an Indian writer has the urge to do his creative work in English, he is obviously convinced that he can give his best through the medium of the foreign tongue.

Bhattacharya is admittedly, and justifiably, sensitive to the charge that Indian authors write in English in order to find easy access to publication and to reap the fat rewards of a world market. To this he replies with the strength of experience and a knowledge of hard facts:

Our novels have to be in the thick of a break-neck race with thousands of Western works. It has been roughly estimated that out of about a hundred book manuscripts received in an American publisher's office, hardly more than one gets into print. To be that one in a hundred the Indian work has to stand in decisive superiority over not only the mass of American manuscripts on the publisher's desk but piles of others from several Continents. . . . In point of fact, an American or British novel has better possibilities in its own home market than an Indian work of equal merit. The foreign publishers' bias, fed by their sales departments, is indeed strongly against Indian material. With soaring production costs, why should they invest money in a venture that is all too uncertain?

He concludes with a reassertion of the validity and genuineness of Indian writing in English.

IV   *Indian Cavalcade*

As has been said, Bhattacharya has written an impressive number of short stories, sketches, and tales. Many have been translated into other languages and a number have appeared in anthologies from India, to England, to Australia. The comments here will be based on two collections of the short fiction that have been published in book format.

In 1948 Nalanda Publications, Bombay, brought out a volume of over thirty sketches under the title *Indian Cavalcade (Some Memorable Yesterdays)*. Bhattacharya indicates the pieces first appeared in several Indian journals. In them the author presents glimpses of his country's past from the Vikram era (ca. 58 B.C.) in North India to a subject nation on the threshold of World War I.

The substance of *Cavalcade* might have proved deadly didactic coming from another pen, but the artistry of the storyteller lends lustre to this re-telling of the history of a people by way of character and incident. Although all Bhattacharya's novels have a sure sense of historical setting, it is in this pilgrimage through two thousand years that we get the fullest sense of the author's training as an historian—a training that has lent validity and power to all the creations of his fertile imagination. In these early writings scholarly training and creative ability unite to imbue past fact with the breath of life. History is, after all, people. And people of any period may be shown living out their flesh and blood experiences in their personal "here and now." By individualizing historical records Bhattacharya lifts from the dusty pages of the past a sense of living immediacy.

A few examples will emphasize our point.[8]

Half a dozen of the thirty-seven pieces are devoted to episodes in the lives of some of India's great women. One such is "A Queen's Dilemma," which opens with a quotation from the record, followed a page or two later by a typical Bhattacharya "come on" paragraph:

"A great sovereign she was, and sagacious, just, beneficent, a patron of the learned, a disposer of justice, a cherisher of her subjects, of warlike talent, endowed with all the admirable attributes of a king." So wrote a contemporary chronicler about Razyia, the eldest daughter and successor of Iltumish, who was the real founder of the Pathan dynasty at Delhi. And the chronicler added (with a sour smile, perhaps, mingled with a sigh): "But as she did not attain the destiny, in her creation, of being computed among men, of what advantage were all these excellent qualifications to her?" . . . (25)

Yet Queen Razyia was a woman of strange passions, and her love for an Abyssinian slave attached to the palace cost her the Delhi throne. (26)

"Pirates from Arakan" opens with a careful setting of place:

Midnight on the Megha. The dark river mingled with the sky, gloom upon gloom. The village lay tucked in sleep. In daytime it was a monochrome in green, with long stretches of growing corn, bamboos, banana clumps, toddy-palms. Ponds were everywhere. With each pond as the central feature was a loose cluster of mud-walled cottages topped by conical straw-padded roofs. And somewhere was the inevitable gray old temple, housing a god, or a goddess, of the people. . . .

Upon this village of Bengal came Terror. Terror unknown in all its history.

A dog barked suddenly in the moonless dark. Another. In a moment a dozen dogs were barking hard, pouring alarm. Some more moments passed. A dismal voice was heard crying out, "The Feringhees! The Feringhees come, the Feringhees!" Shrieks crossed the village, end to end. Men darted out madly with women and children, flying through the night into the fields, hiding in ditches and thickets and behind the waving corn. A few breathless minutes, and the village lay deserted, dead. (81)

It is against this background that the reader is introduced to the coming of the Portuguese early in the sixteenth century for trade in goods and people. (Only in 1961 were these last "Feringhees," who had remained as colonial exploiters, forcibly evicted from their Goa pocket near Bombay.)

"The Black Hole of Calcutta" is so notorious in the annals of world history that it has found its way even into dictionary definition: "A small cell in which, allegedly, 146 British subjects were confined on June 20, 1756, of whom 123 died of asphyxia" (*Standard College Dictionary*). Bhattacharya's account of this barbarous event begins with an introduction of the reputed perpetrator of the infamy:

> Siraj-ud-Daula burst into uncontrollable fury. "Go!" his voice hissed to the cowering messengers. Fiercely he paced the room, as he watched them withdraw in fear and humility. "Those vile traders, those sons of pigs!"
> In a while he cooled off, sat on a divan and gulped down a glass of sparkling Persian wine. He was wearing a white, flowing robe, close-fitting to the arms, and a coloured girdle of twisted silk; three rows of pearls on his chest; a turban shaped like a skull-cap and set with gems. (151)

After a dramatic picture of the night of horror, the author then raises the question of the veracity of the record:

> But was there really a Black Hole horror? Or was it a fabrication? Strange falsehoods creep sometimes into history and grow hardened, defying the disapproval of research. It is just possible that the event never took place. It is probable that its horrors have been fantastically exaggerated. . . .
> The world came to know of the incident from the account written by Holwell, who had been a prisoner that fatal night and had survived. But Holwell was, on clear evidence, an incorrigible liar. . . . (155)

Bhattacharya returns to and ends with the personality of the unfortunate Siraj-ud-Daula, whom he pictures as kindly and no match for General Clive, England's "arch conspirator."

Finally, in "A Moment in the Mutiny" Bhattacharya brings his mastery of description to play in making real one of the bloodiest clashes between the British *raj* and the Indian people. In the pages of British history the confrontation is called "The Indian Mutiny" or "The Sepoy Rebellion"—that is, the rebellion of the Indian soldiers serving in the British army. With pride, Indian historians refer to the 1857 conflict as the "War of Independence." Here is the storyteller's introduction to a noted episode in Indian history:

> There was no moon, but the sky was bejewelled with stars. A night in mid-September. Two British engineer officers accompanied by a number of picked riflemen halted at the edge of a jungle.
> The fortifications of Delhi loomed ahead—walls intersected with towers and bastioned fronts, mounted with guns. . . . At the edge of the jungle were planted British batteries, belching a destructive fire on the enemy defences.

... The besiegers were determined to take Delhi, for without it the Indian Empire was lost. The besieged were bent on defending it, for with Delhi as the storm centre of their movement the war of independence might be won.

Two engineer officers, Medley and Lang, crept through the starry night towards the Kashmere bastion. They were out to examine a breach at close range and ascertain whether it would let in storming columns. . . . Their hearts beat quickly as they saw that the breach in the wall was wide, un-protected by guns in the flanks, and that the slope of the ditch was easy of ascent.

Their report decided the course of events. . . . (207–208)

So is related that beginning of the end of the 1857 attempt for an independence that would not come for ninety years.

In a postscript, which he entitles "The Supreme Moment," Bhat-tacharya quotes from a talk by Jawaharlal Nehru on the occasion of India's achievement of national sovereignity. Again, the context is effectively set:

A deepening night of mid-August. Jawaharlal Nehru addresses the Con-stituent Assembly of India in session at the capital. And as he speaks, a proud empire passes away and a new world force rises, a great people's republic comes into being. India is re-born. (259)

So England and India go their independent but generally con-cordant ways:

So the Indian cavalcade in its aureole of vivid history divides itself at the supreme moment and the twain on their separate paths move on towards blue horizons ahead. The freedom to be Free. . . . The challenge of the future. . . . The tryst with destiny. (261)

V *Steel Hawk and Other Stories*

The slight stories of the *Steel Hawk* collection have to do largely with village life and views. Several are "short shorts" of no more than three or four pages, essentially brief character sketches. To the Bhattacharya reader their interest may reside not so much in the intrinsic value of the stories as in their indication that the author is more at ease in the novel than in the short story form. Too often situations appear contrived and dialogue strained, suggesting a weight of meaning not borne out by the basic content. Yet, as was said earlier, Bhattacharya's stories have been published widely and in many languages.

Of the fifteen stories that make up this 143-page pocket-size book, three seem to me to come closest to the level of the teller's longer works. "My Brave Great-Uncle," "Pilgrims in Uniform," and "The Faltering Pendulum" are warm with village character and rich in cultural insights.

The protagonist of the first story is the great-uncle of a village friend of the narrator. He believes in spirits. Especially he believes that his dead wife is always near him observing all he does, this despite the fact that she has been given the Hindu rites that are supposed to have put the spirit to rest. Great-Uncle has built up a reputation for courage, living as he does apparently without fear of the spirits he believes surround him.

When a Brahmin priest dies, it is natural that the old man should be chosen to guard his bier through the night. But Great-Uncle bursts from the room in abject fear an hour later, and a village myth is shattered.

The story is poetic in style, with a suggestion of the rhythm of village speech. The character of the old man is believable and appealing.

"Pilgrims in Uniform" has to do with the annual pilgrimage to the holy city of Jaganath for the Car Festival. A young novitiate priest has succeeded in rounding up two score pilgrims to go with him. He gives them a sense of community by having their clothes dyed saffron color (the "uniform" of the title). A city man who shares their train compartment derides their faith as a "philosophy of opium" causing them to be "drugged with fatalism."

In the group is a young boy who has come, not as a pilgrim, but as a thief. When he hears the young priest refute the scoffer by enunciating the power of thought which helps the believer to see beauty and truth—to see the Lord—the thief is purified.

Here, again, the style suggests the peasant mind and reveals considerable religious conviction.

"The Faltering Pendulum" captures in a central episode the final barren years of a lonely old village woman whose physical and emotional life is dependent upon a pumpkin vine and a young goat. The goat "youngling" becomes the rag-woman's constant companion, her one warm bond with another life; the pumpkin vine her promise of sustenance. Typical of the author is the ironic turn at the conclusion of the story when the goat's attack upon the apparently barren pumpkin vine leads to the animal's destruction and the revelation of the vine's productivity:

> The goat had cleared up thick patches of leaves, and on a stripped tendril a tiny pumpkin hung. Another, a yard away. Oh, how could she have missed them?
> Even in her deep anguish the rag-woman's tear-stained face beamed. The goat was dead, a white heap still lying on the mud floor. But the pumpkin vines had sprung to fruitful life, after their long barren dead-aliveness. . . .[9]

Several stories are told in the impressionistic style of the earlier Bhattacharya. The characterization of "Public Figure," for instance, in a story of that title, is frankly stereotyped rather than personalized. This incident and the central characters are especially interesting, however, in view of their having been transferred almost whole-cloth to Bhattacharya's fifth novel, *Shadow from Ladakh*. There is an intensification of interest in *Shadow*, where the central character is changed to one of Bhattacharya's strong, "activist" women. Here the character is fully developed and personalized, and the action is not only consistent with that character but helps to reveal it.

In "Public Figure" a father, who heads a fund-raising drive, hits upon the idea of having his daughter publicly contribute some of her gold jewelry to the cause. The cause will be promoted, he believes, and the resultant publicity will enhance his public image. In *Shadow from Ladakh* the promotional scheme is devised by the girl's mother, who is one of the caricatured country club matrons of the novel, and is presented with considerable humor and psychological insight.

"Glory at Twilight" concerns a now-ruined banker who is slyly outdone by his wily uncle when he returns to his native village for the wedding of the uncle's daughter.

"Steel Hawk," the volume's title story, has the ingredients for a first-rate tale but doesn't quite come off. Too much of the telling is by way of recapitulation and through the speech of the grandson of the old peasant woman whose point of view is central to both the present and past events. Nothing seems to be achieved by keeping Grandma herself from viewing and reacting to the airplane—the strange "steel hawk"—that has come down in a village field, just as she, a teenage bride, had viewed and reacted to the first train to come through the countryside. Having the grandson see and speak for her makes the incident seem detached, cold, and remote.

The remaining stories—"The Acrobats," "The Quack," "She, Born of Light," "A Moment of Eternity," "Lattu Ram's Adventure," and "Pictures in the Fire"—are all essentially character sketches. They range in effectiveness from the touching "Moment of Eternity," in which a widowed mother in desperation kills her children and then attempts to take her own life, to "She, Born of Light," which is uncomfortably artificial and *précieux*, the point of view shifting awkwardly and confusingly in the limited space of a short story. "Mere Monkeys" captures some authentic observations of simian communal behavior, though one wonders whether the denouement is more anthropomorphic than zoologically descriptive.

CHAPTER 9

Translator/Editor/Biographer

BHABANI BHATTACHARYA, creative writer, has resisted efforts to entice him down other writing trails. His term (1949–50) as Press Attaché with the Indian Embassy in Washington required regular meetings with the American press, the editing of a weekly bulletin of news from India, and news briefings of Ambassador Vijaya Lakshmi Pandit (Prime Minister Nehru's sister). Though the year provided exciting and stimulating experiences, it was generally a frustrating and unhappy one for him. He has said bluntly, "I disliked it. I got no creative writing done."

Back in India he signed a three-year contract as assistant editor of the *Illustrated Weekly of India*, published in Bombay. India's equivalent of *Life* magazine, with its mass circulation, obviously was not Bhattacharya's métier—especially when he found himself saddled with its business operations during the manager's extended absence. And so, when invited to be a member of India's first Cultural Delegation to Russia (1951) Bhattacharya felt no hesitancy in dropping a two-month editorial schedule in order to go. Nor did he hesitate, on his return, in resigning from the position as assistant editor a full year before the contract period was up. This, too, had been a writer's experience that was at counter purposes with the central core of his being.

I *Discovery of Self*

The invitation from the Union of Soviet Writers had come on the heels of the publication of *So Many Hungers!* in Russian translation. Bhattacharya says the six-week visit in the Soviet Union was in a way a realization of himself as an author. "For the first time I saw it was very prestigious to be a writer," he told me.[1] People pressed about him with their autograph books. He told about an experience at the Bolshoi Theatre that was pure self-revelation:

> Suddenly I found the whole audience clapping and cheering. "Do you know whom they are cheering?" I was asked. "No," I replied. "They are cheering you. You must return their applause," I was told.

Even on the collective farms he found he was known. And he was convinced the response to him had not been "stage managed"; that people had really read his books. In Russia he spoke on the radio for the first time, making a five-minute recording for which he was paid 500 rubles. When he asked why he was being paid for so slight a thing he was told: "We are not paying you just for your talk, but for what you have made of yourself. Behind your talk is a lifetime of literary striving, and we are honoring that." And his mind is still boggled by the "fantastic amount" he was paid by the *Literanaya Gazetta* for an article on how he came to write *So Many Hungers!*

He met many writers in Georgia, where there is a rich literary tradition. In fact, he was with Russian authors throughout his visit. One of the most moving experiences for him was his visit to Tolstoy's home at Yasnaya Polyana, south of Moscow. He refers peripherally to this in *Gandhi the Writer* when he comments on the relationship between Gandhi and Tolstoy.

After Russia and subsequent stops in Prague, Rome, and Paris, the news job at the *Illustrated Weekly* appeared even more drab than before he left. Besides, though the *Weekly* wanted articles on the Russian trip, Bhattacharya found they expected to dictate how his experiences should be presented—essentially with an anti-Russian bias. As a result, Bhattacharya declined to write at all, and within three or four months he had resigned.

There is reason to believe that it was not so much the disagreement with the management that brought the resignation as that the entire Russia trip had been a journey in self-discovery. Bhattacharya returned home fired with renewed ambition as a creative writer. Soon after leaving the *Illustrated Weekly*, *Music for Mohini* appeared. Thereafter there would be no return to full-time journalism or editing.

II *Tagore Translator and Editor*

Nothing more tellingly testifies to his love for Rabindranath Tagore than Bhattacharya's early translations of several score of Tagore's vignettes and his later service as chief editor and translator of a collection of essays by Tagore. The two "labors of love" mark opposite poles of Bhattacharya's life and writing career—the translations first appearing in the *London Spectator* when he was a young student in England, while the editing came at the apex of his career as a creative artist.

As we think of Bhattacharya in this new role, it would be both pertinent and interesting to consider his relationship to one of the great creative minds of all time. In several conversations I have had with the author, he has spoken with genuine emotion of his acquaintance with Tagore.

Young Bhabani Bhattacharya went to Tagore's school, Santiniketan, near Bolpur, on the plains of West Bhagirath northwest of Calcutta, several times during his student days. However, it was not until his first years in London that he actually met the man who was then recognized as the greatest literary figure of Asia. "I saw him from a distance during my student days," he recounted. "Although he was very approachable, I didn't dare approach him. I have never seen anyone else who had his dazzling personality. As one is dazed on looking at the sun, so I felt in his presence." One gathers that after the overture was made, however, a mutual respect and attraction was recognized.

On a trip to Berlin later, Bhattacharya met Tagore there and once again in London before the great man returned to his native Bengal. When after several years Bhattacharya went back to India, Tagore suggested he come as a professor to Viswabharati, his world university which had opened in 1921. But Bhattacharya had tried his literary wings in the meantime and was beginning to envision a creative career of his own. Although he was flattered by the invitation, which bordered on insistence, he refused. "I felt," he says, "that I would continue merely to be dazzled by him and would write in his mode and under his influence." He saw a basic difference in styles and purposes, regarding himself as a "Realist" and Tagore as a "Romanticist."

We recognize, then, that Tagore in a manner blessed Bhattacharya as his translator. There is also evidence that he would have had confidence in the critical judgment that guided Bhattacharya as editor with a final voice in the selection of the essays most worthy of perpetuation in an internationally published collection. For Bhattacharya has said that Tagore wrote to him, still a college undergraduate, in praise of an article of literary criticism he had published in a Bengali magazine.

III   *The Golden Boat*

The mixed collection, given the title *The Golden Boat*, was brought out in book form in London, in 1932. The first Indian edition appeared under the Jaico imprint in 1956. By 1964 the 114-page pocket-sized book had entered its third edition.

In a translator's note, Bhattacharya tells how the title was determined:

> I should perhaps mention that *The Golden Boat* is not an English rendering of *Sonar Tori*, the volume of verses that has given the present work its title. The selection covers a number of Tagore's books. *The Golden Boat* carries gleanings from many fields. That is the significance of its name.
>
> I vividly remember a springtime day in London when the Poet, then on one of his periodic visits to Europe, gave me his approval of the English translation, the typescript of which he had just read. I asked him to give a name to the volume.
>
> "Silhouettes?" he suggested, without conviction.
>
> I was not happy. I hesitated.
>
> "*The Golden Boat*?" I ventured.
>
> The Poet reflected awhile. "That's it," he said and his smile was warm.[2]

It might be added that the title agreed upon had surfaced some years earlier (1908) in an essay by Tagore, "East and West," in which he presented a compressed view of India's history vis-à-vis the impact of the West. With a poet's diction, he refers there to "the golden boat of Time."

Although this slim book is composed of the translated work of another writer, it nevertheless adds in several respects to our view of Bhattacharya himself.

First, the translations come through successfully in English. Sentences are direct and uncluttered; idiomatic expressions are often an intriguing Anglo-Indian blend that helps to carry both setting and cultural flavor to the non-Indian reader. From Tagore's approval of the results, we are assured that Bhattacharya's personal writing style has not obtruded on that of the original author.

Then, what is omitted and what is included in the concise four-page "profile" of Tagore gives evidence of Bhattacharya's own concerns. It is significant that in so brief a résumé he takes time to dwell on Tagore's catholicity of interests and abilities and his dedication to a "union" between East and West, for these are prevailing themes running through all Bhattacharya's own creative writing.

He was resolved to work not only for a co-ordination between India's past
and present, a fusion of the best elements, but also for a synthesis of the East
with the West, a "union" between them. Western materialism, he believed,
had to be tempered with "creative ideas" from the East. And the inwardness
of the East had to be supplemented with the Western genius for social orga-
nization. The world could not afford to remain split forever into the Orient
and the Occident. (9)

Finally, is it mere chance that dictated the opening of the collection with "Tell Me a Story" in which the creative writer is likened
to the divine Creator?

The well-wishers have never cared to think clearly over one point: that, to
compose stories has been a hobby of the Creator Himself. Unless you shake
this habit out of the Creator, you cannot shake it out of mankind.
   Once upon a time, in His busy workshop, the Creator began to build out of
the elements. . . . Ages passed. At last, one day the Creator made man. Up to
that time He had been partly a scientist and partly an architect; now He became a literary artist.
   He began to unfold the human soul through fiction. . . . History and story
combine to make our world. . . . To man a figure of the myths is as real as a
figure of history. The point is, not which is the more reliable fact, but which is
the more enjoyable fiction. . . . (15–16)

IV   *Rabindranath Tagore's Social Essays*

Towards Universal Man, a volume of essays by Rabindranath
Tagore, was undertaken by Bhattacharya on assignment from the
Tagore Commemorative Volume Society and under a grant from
the Ford Foundation to mark the centennial (1961) of the Nobel
Prize poet's birth. A truly international enterprise, the book was
published simultaneously in India, the United Kingdom, and the
United States by the Asia Publishing House, and immediately translated into the languages of France, Italy, Russia, and Yugoslavia.
   It was pure consecration that led the creative writer to take on the
arduous chores involved in serving as "Editor-cum-Chief Translator" of this pioneer collection of some of Tagore's finest writings
on contemporary social problems. Bhattacharya worked with three
dozen of India's top minds in winnowing masses of previously
unpublished prose writing in selecting the eighteen essays that com-
prise the commemorative volume. He was one of ten translators

and the one charged with responsibility for the final polish put on all the essays as they ultimately appeared in print.

When Indian scholars and translators had selected thirty items as "finalists" in the running, Dr. Bhattacharya then submitted the English translations to nineteen well-known foreign intellectuals with the request that they vote for the twenty that seemed to them best. Among those so consulted were Lord Hailsham, British Cabinet Minister; Malcolm Macdonald, United Kingdom High Commissioner to India; Mrs. Alva Myrdal, Ambassador from Sweden; Norman Cousins, editor of the American weekly, *Saturday Review*; Dr. Mordecai Johnson, President of Howard University, one of the most highly respected of America's Negro educators; and Dr. B. Gofurov, Director of the Institute of Orientology, Moscow. In such fashion, then, the final selection of eighteen essays was arrived at.

In his preface to the collection Humayun Kabir, then India's Minister for Culture and Scientific Research and chairman of the Commemorative Society, referred to Bhattacharya as "one of the best-known Indian writers in English" and commended his diligence in going over "the text of every essay and helping in editing and re-editing them in order to bring the English as close to Tagore's thought as possible."

Towards Universal Man offers a panorama of Tagore's views on a diversity of subjects covering a half-century of time. Humayun Kabir points out that, although "Tagore has been universally recognized as one of the greatest lyric poets of all times . . . it is however not so well known that [he] made major contributions in the fields of education, economics, politics, and social affairs—contributions that are significant not only for India but the whole world." The centenary volume seeks to bring some of these lesser-known contributions to a broader public.

The volume is also of value to those of us who seek to evaluate the contribution of Bhabani Bhattacharya to India and the world. His major involvement in its realization brings to full circle his participation in the life of his "literary *guru*" and presents affirmation of the novelist's competency in other publishing spheres.

V *Gandhi Biographer*

The writing of biography is clearly not the first love of the creative writer. Why, then, should novelist Bhabani Bhattacharya have undertaken to add to the multiplicity of Gandhi biographies already written? The full title of his book, published in 1969, offers one clue—*Gandhi the Writer: The Image As It Grew*. Bhattacharya the writer is interested in Gandhi as the writer and in revealing this one particular facet of a multi-faceted career. This also was the interest of the Ford Foundation "whose financial assistance," Bhattacharya says in his acknowledgments, "made it possible for me to work uninterruptedly on this volume."

The second motivation is found in Bhattacharya's devotion to Gandhi, the man, the *guru*, the martyr; presenting here the other face of the same coin that bears the imprint of Tagore. Pertinent is the point Bhattacharya makes in regard to the French novelist Romain Rolland's writing on the life of the Mahatma:

> ... Were Gandhi simply an idealist, Rolland would not have gone out of his own domain—creative writing—to bring into the literary horizon a personality that had few points of contact with his own. But Gandhi had transformed a vision into reality. He had turned a nebulous idea into an iron-hard technique and was applying it for social and political ends on a massive scale—millions of men and women were involved in this epochal "experiment." (160)[3]

As has been said, the special challenge to Bhattacharya, coming after a long line of distinguished biographers, is to assess the *writer* rather than the whole man. Or, perhaps I should say—more especially than to assess the man. For, by the time he has completed his 350-page survey, Bhattacharya has covered all major factors of a complicated life and character, though not in the biographer's usual chronological progression.

VI   *The Writer's Art*

> ... There is a genre of writing which owes its enrichment to truth, not to beauty. The words, the clay of creativity, mean almost nothing in their own individual or collective right, acting only as the instrument of a certain planned purpose. It is the nature and dimension of that purpose that make a dividing line (sharp here, blurred there) between the writer and the non-writer.
>
> No one who has used the stuff of words on a massive scale has been as passionately purposive as Gandhi. No one has used words with such intense longing to be down-to-earth on the one hand and, paradoxically, to reach for the stars on the other. (2)

So writes the novelist concerning the lawyer-statesman turned author.

Again and again Bhattacharya, in his comments on Gandhi's writing art, reveals his personal author's philosophy. Let us look at some of the most revealing.

A writer is his thought, his dream, his dedication. Provided, of course, that he gives all these an outer habitation in terms of language. That is a compulsion he lives for. Without that, he could be an idealist, a man of wisdom, a seer, but certainly not a writer. (2)

[Of Gandhi's Gujerati reinterpretation of the *Bhagavad Gita*] His style is clear, lucid, precise, full of concentrated directness; it is stripped of rhetoric and the varied modes of sophistication.... (85)

[As a journalist, Gandhi had developed] a business-like prose style: simple, straightforward, orderly, precise; well reasoned, lucid, adequately condensed; and above all else, single-minded, persuasive. (105)

From this base Bhattacharya comments that Gandhi's writing became "power-packed" and assumed a quality that "could set the reader's blood afire." He notes this was particularly striking at that time, since Indian writing in English tended to be ostentatious and ornate.

We sense approval in Bhattacharya's relating the agreement of Rolland and Gandhi on the purposes of art:

Like Tolstoy, they refuted the concept of "art for art's sake." "For me, all art must be based on truth," Gandhi said. "I reject beautiful things, if instead of expressing truth, they express untruth. I accept the formula 'Art brings joy and is good,' but on the condition I mentioned." (164)

Another responsive chord is found in Gandhi's refusal to give up the English edition of his weekly newspaper, *Harijan*, for some of Bhattacharya's bitterest critics have been those who censure him for writing in English rather than Bengali, his "mother tongue." In response to a correspondent who urged that he drop the English edition of his paper, Gandhi replied:

"I cannot stop the English edition.... My relations with the West are increasing every day.... I cannot cast out the English language from my small store of knowledge. I do not wish to forget that language, nor do I wish all Indians to give up or forget it.... English [is] the language of the world. Its international position cannot be disputed. Imperialist rule of the Englishman will go, because it was and is an evil. But the superior role of the English language cannot go." (193)

Later, Bhattacharya returns to the subject, using much the same arguments he would use to his own critics:

The major part of his writing had to be in English. Through English alone could Gandhi reach all the corners of the Indian subcontinent across the linguistic frontiers. (224)

In a chapter evaluating Gandhi's impact on Indian literature, Bhattacharya cites the "new direction" he set for the writers of his time:

Inspired by him, they turned towards the depiction of the life of the common man, the poor and the illiterate, particularly in the villages. Their prose style became less ornamental, less designed for the highbrow scholar. Simple, direct, natural, the literature of the Gandhian era aimed at appealing not to the classes alone, but to the masses as well. . . . There was a reaction against obsolete values. The writers drew largely on life for their themes and new horizons opened up before them. (228–29)

Appropriately, Bhattacharya includes himself among the approximately 140 poets, novelists, and biographers whose works either deal directly with Gandhi's life or who reflect his ideas and ideals. *So Many Hungers!* and *Shadow from Ladakh* are mentioned as catching the "accents of the Gandhian Age," as Srinivasa Iyengar put it. However, all Bhattacharya's major works are rooted in a similar philosophy, and surely all deal predominantly with "the common man" in a "simple, direct, and natural" manner.

VII *Direct Reflections*

Apart from these generalized agreements in purpose and in approach to writing, there are a number of striking specific ideas that are reflected in incidents and metaphoric concepts in Bhattacharya's own works. One such is found in the following quotation from Gandhi's personal addendum to his Gujerati version of Ruskin's *Unto This Last*:

India must indeed have Swaraj ("Freedom") but she must have it by righteous methods. Our Swaraj must be real Swaraj. India was once a golden land, because Indians then had a heart of gold. The land is still the same but is a desert because we are corrupt. It can become a land of gold again only if the base metal of our present national character is transmuted into gold. The philosopher's stone which can effect this transformation is a little word of two syllables, Satya ("Truth"). If every Indian sticks to truth, Swaraj will come to us of its own accord. (36)

The idea of the "philosopher's stone" that can transmute base metal into gold becomes the metaphor central to *A Goddess Named Gold*. In Bhattacharya's novel the "philosopher's stone" becomes Meera's *taveez*, given her in good faith by her grandfather but corrupted in its unrighteous use. Whereas the touchstone for Gandhi is *Satya* (Truth), for Bhattacharya it is *Swaraj* itself—Freedom based on righteousness. Compare with the above passage the message of the minstrel grandfather as he addresses the villagers gathered about him on the eve of Independence, after the evil of the misused *taveez* has spent its course:

This day with its great gift for India's people—a touchstone! He paused, allowing the hum of astonished comments to stop. Freedom was the touchstone, he resumed, his voice stronger. It was a touchstone for everyone. To possess this touchstone was not enough, for it could wake to life and work its miracle only when acts of faith were done.

His words grew in power. "Brothers, now that we have freedom, we need acts of faith. Then only will there be a transmutation. Friends, then only will our lives turn into gold. Without acts of faith, freedom is a dead pebble tied to the arm with a bit of string, fit only to be cast into the river."[4]

No book, however, more directly reflects Gandhi's influence on Bhattacharya, the writer, than *Shadow from Ladakh* in which the protagonist, Satyajit, struggles to be a Gandhi in a new time, living in terms of complete chastity, voluntary poverty, unwavering truth (in this connection, note the root meaning of his name), and fearlessness. Gandhigram is modeled on Gandhi's Sevagram ("village dedicated to service"). The detailed description of its appearance and of the life lived there may be seen as an almost factual representation of Sevagram itself. It is one of the many elements that give *Shadow from Ladakh* the ring of authenticity.

The pivotal, climactic action at the close of the Ladakh drama—Satyajit's pathetically aborted march to the disputed valley—in both the author's mind and his character's dream is patterned on Gandhi's "historic march to Dandi village on the sea-coast, with 79 inmates

of Sabarmati Ashram, to break the salt law and initiate the Satyagraha struggle." (292) This act of civil disobedience in protest
against the colonial government's tax on salt, which affected India's
rich and poor alike, led to the arrest of some 100,000 men and women
who followed in Gandhi's footsteps to the sea. The total drama
catalyzed public opinion throughout the world in favor of Gandhi's
protest. A full year passed between that March day in 1930 and the
lifting of the oppressive law, but the sluggish wheels of justice had
been turned by peaceful means, not violent.

   Satyajit aspires to settle the Ladakh conflict in similar fashion:

I have been blessed by close contact with Gandhi-ji over the years, said
Satyajit to himself. In this crisis I will act as he would have acted, even though
I am less than his shadow. I will tread on the footprints he has left.[5]
   "I will take a Shanti Sena—to the disputed regions in Ladakh," [he later
informs his wife Suruchi]. . . .
   "The Peace Mission will pass across the mountain ranges, along the deep
valleys, and reach the frontier between India and China. . . . The demand for
peace will be our only weapon. And faith in the spirit of man our only shield.". . .
   Suruchi said, "The members of the Mission will be drawn from all over
India?"
   "No . . . the response will become international. That's how a world moral
force will bestride Ladakh. No brute force can prevail against that power, the
roused conscience of man. And at the end of it all . . . two great Asian peoples
will find back their lost heritage of friendship. The brief aberration will be
forgotten."[6]

   When Chinese forces encroach as far as the borders of Assam,
Satyajit determines the moment for the march has come. Ironically—but consistent with the characterization of his protagonist—
Bhattacharya times this decision to coincide with China's unan-
nounced and totally unexpected ceasefire. So it is that the "present-
day Gandhi" is thwarted by the elements of history as well as by the
elements of his own character which had failed to enlist more than a
sparse following for his catalytic call.

VIII   *"Soul Brothers"*

   Throughout *Gandhi the Writer* one who has read Bhattacharya's
novels is aware of the deep and abiding influence Gandhi's personality, way of life, and philosophy have had on him. Although Bhattacharya did not have as close a personal relationship with Gandhi

as he had had with Tagore, Gandhiji is obviously more truly his "soul brother" than is Tagore. The multi-talented, brilliant, impressively handsome Tagore—though his fellow Brahmin Bengali—would always remain awe-inspiring and "dazzling," to use Bhattacharya's own term. The quiet, unassuming, humble, yet firm and determined Gandhi, born on the opposite shores of the country, of another language and caste, would have stronger appeal and develop closer ties, differences notwithstanding.

Perhaps because of the focus on Gandhi as a writer, the biographer's personal responses to his subject are more evident than they might be in a formal, supposedly "objective," biography. In fact, one of the fascinations of Bhattacharya's view of Gandhi as a world figure is the fresh focus and added perspective afforded those who have read other biographies or Gandhi's writings on himself. Some of the achievements and associations most famous in history become peripheral in this approach, and others surface with unique emphasis; witness Gandhi's widely reported meetings with such British leaders as Winston Churchill (who once referred to him as "that half-naked fakir"), Lord Bracken ("Gandhi should be kept in jail"), Indian Viceroy Lord Irwin, and others. These political celebrities step backstage, while coming front center are Ralph Waldo Emerson, Romain Rolland, the American theologian John Haynes Holmes, Leo Tolstoy, and even Charlie Chaplin. It is refreshing to find Churchill mentioned only in passing, although several pages are given to Gandhi's meeting with Charlie Chaplin in London. Gandhi's hostess, Muriel Lester, observed Gandhi and Chaplin as they "sat on a couch, rather apart from the rest of us, and talked about the people, the toilers, the underfed, the machine slaves and the imprisoned." (147)

We get a good sense of Bhattacharya's personal priorities in the considerable space he gives to the impact of Gandhi on two of Europe's greatest novelists whose writings were inspired by humanistic concern—Romain Rolland and Leo Tolstoy. Both appear again and again in the course of the book. We see these two as Gandhi's "soul brothers," as also they undoubtedly are Bhattacharya's.

At the very outset, Bhattacharya refers to Gandhi's being "overwhelmed" by Tolstoy's *The Kingdom of God Is Within You* and other of his religious writings with their emphasis on "universal love." The New Testament teaching—"Resist not him that is evil, but whomsoever smiteth thee on thy right cheek, turn to him the other."—according to Bhattacharya, came to Gandhi through Tolstoy's book combining with the message of the *Bhagavad Gita* to become the motivating force in Gandhi's non-violence. (55)

During his years in South Africa, Gandhi formulated his passive resistance philosophy and gave it the first practical test. He founded Tolstoy Farm near Johannesburg, and from there he entered into an extensive correspondence with Tolstoy, which continued until the Russian philosopher-novelist's death in 1910. Bhattacharya writes:

> Many years after the death of Tolstoy, Gandhi stated: "Russia gave me in Tolstoy a teacher who furnished a reasoned basis for my non-violence. Tolstoy blessed my movement in South Africa when it was still in its infancy and of whose wonderful possibilities I had yet to learn. It was he who had prophesied in his letter to me that I was leading a movement which was destined to bring a message of hope to the downtrodden peoples of the earth. . . . Tolstoy was the greatest apostle of non-violence that the present age has produced." (72)

Bhattacharya interjects a personal observation on Tolstoy's long-time interest in India, pre-dating his spiritual affiliation with Gandhi:

> Perhaps it was no accident of history that a wealthy Russian aristocrat, who was also the author of the greatest novels in world literature, was being tormented by the same spiritual problems that the unknown Indian in South Africa faced. Tolstoy's interest in India was deep-rooted; I found ample evidence of it on the bookshelves of the library of his ancestral home in Yasnaya Polyana—a village some 130 miles south of Moscow—when I visited it some years ago. Indian journals dating back to the first decade of this century . . . were a pleasant surprise indeed.
>
> Immortalized by his novels, Count Leo Tolstoy was vested with a second personality, worlds apart from the creative artist. The other Tolstoy, the seeker of spiritual truths, one of the greatest thinkers of all time, drew Gandhi's intense interest and homage. It was not Tolstoy's writings alone; equally dynamic was the example he set by the reorientation of life that he adopted. (66–67)

Later, Bhattacharya refers to entries in Tolstoy's diary in which he speaks of Gandhi's letters, and of reading "Gandhi on Civilization; wonderful." Tolstoy also noted his reading a book about the Indian *guru* that he judged "very important." Bhattacharya observes that in a letter to a friend Tolstoy spoke of Gandhi as "a person very close to us, to me." In his last letter to Gandhi, which arrived in South Africa after its writer's death, Tolstoy said:

> The more I live—and specially now that I am approaching death—the more I feel inclined to express to others the feelings which so strongly move my being.

What one calls non-resistance is in reality nothing else but the discipline of love. . . . Love is the supreme law of life. . . .

Therefore, your work in the Transvaal, which seems to be so far away from the centre of our world, is the most essential work, the most important of all the work now being done in the world. . . . (70–71)

Bhattacharya also reviews the spiritual affiliation that developed between the pacifist French novelist, Romain Rolland, and Gandhi. Rolland is first mentioned in the biography during Bhattacharya's discussion of a disagreement between Tagore and Gandhi as to the possible divisiveness of Gandhi's *Satyagraha* movement, which Tagore saw as "a doctrine of negation and despair, narrowness and exclusiveness" that would "taint India's honour in the eyes of the world." (100)

Rolland entered the controversy between India's two great luminaries as it broke into published letters, essays, and verses. Tagore's poem, "The Call of Truth," acknowledged the clarion that consecrated self-sacrifice to the rebirth of a nation. But would it "only obscure the greater world from our view"? (101) Gandhi, in a responsive article, "The Great Sentinel," his title for Tagore, concluded the exchange:

I have found it impossible to soothe suffering patients with a song from Kabir. The hungry millions ask for one poem—invigorating food. They cannot be given it. They must earn it. And they can earn it only by the sweat of their brow. (102)

Romain Rolland, who admired both, "called 'The Call of Truth' a poem of sunlight. 'The Great Sentinel' made him think of a Bodhisattva, who had gone to live with the disinherited." (102) The quotation of this European perspective, which selects the common affirmations found in divergent points of view, seems to me indicative of the emphasis on agreement and accommodation that is a prevailing motif in all Bhattacharya's creative work.

Increasingly Rolland reflected the Gandhian influence in his writing and in his active response to the political turmoil in the Europe of his time. In a letter delivered to Gandhi as he arrived in France in 1931, when Rolland himself was ill in Switzerland, he wrote: "The whole question for us now is that this inevitable revolution would be achieved by non-violence and love, and that it should not be left to the blind forces of hatred which would spread destruction on the earth." (142)

Later, during the closing action of *Shadow from Ladakh*, Bhattacharya has one of his characters refer to Rolland's dedication to
the Gandhian principle of non-violence:

Krishnamurti spoke: "Words written by Romain Rolland come to my mind:
'If the India of nonviolence were to go down in the battle, it is Christ himself
who will be pierced by it, with a supreme lance thrust, on the Cross. And this
time there would be no resurrection!' "[7]

Even before he had met Gandhi personally, Rolland had (in 1922)
written one of the first biographies of Gandhi, who was then only
just entering the quarter century that would end in the liberation of
a people and in his own martyrdom. Bhattacharya's personal assessment of Rolland comes as he begins a discussion of Rolland's biography of Gandhi.

It must be recalled that Romain Rolland (1866–1944) himself was as great
a man as Gandhi. His novel *Jean Christophe* had brought him world acclaim
and he received the Nobel Prize for Literature in 1915. . . . A fearless champion
of the oppressed, his humanism had no parallel at the time. In the fury of
nationalist fervour, his ardent appeal for peace was lost. Yet he declared in
his anti-war book, *Above the Battle* (1915): "For one year, I have been rich in
enemies. Let me say this to them: They can hate me, but they will not teach
me to hate."
     His internationalism—a compulsive inheritance from Tolstoy—forced him
into exile from his homeland, France. . . . Romain Rolland saw quickly and
accurately the historic significance of a unique movement that an Indian,
unknown outside his country, had just launched. (159–60)

This reminds us, again, of Bhattacharya's own motivation as author of *Gandhi the Writer*. Bhattacharya goes on to indicate the love
Rolland had for two of the greatest minds and spirits of contemporary India and of their love for each other, despite their disagreement
over means to achieve mutually agreed upon ends. And here again
we hear the note of assent in Bhattacharya's own creative work:

He [Rolland] made a comparison between two great men of East and West,
both of whom he adored. This was in the context of conversations with Tagore.
     Tagore always looked upon Gandhi as a saint, and I have often heard him
speak of him with veneration. When, in referring to the Mahatma, I mentioned Tolstoy, Tagore pointed out to me . . . how much more clothed in
light and radiance Gandhi's spirit is than Tolstoy's. With Gandhi, everything
is nature—modest, simple, pure—while his struggles are hallowed by religious

serenity, whereas with Tolstoy everything is proud revolt against pride, hatred against hatred, passion against passion. Everything in Tolstoy is violence, even his doctrine of non-violence. (161)

So, we gain fresh insights into Gandhi as we view his character through a prism of views from Bhattacharya to Romain Rolland to Leo Tolstoy. Similarly, we gain fresh insights into the character and creative genius of Bhattacharya as he departs from his usual field of fiction to trace—through another writer's art—the course of one man from a seemingly insignificant beginning in the law courts of South Africa to sainthood on the shores of the sacred Ganges.

CHAPTER 10

"The Farther Road"

The lantern which I carry in my hand makes
enemy of the darkness of the farther road.
—Rabindranath Tagore

L OOKING back over Bhabani Bhattacharya's forty years as a
writer, with the benefit of recent events as our viewfinder, we
recognize his forward vision. In many respects Bhattacharya has
been in the vanguard of authors addressing themselves to social
issues. His grounding in cultural history and political science has
helped him, as an artist, to look beyond narrow, temporary problems to issues that surmount time and place.

I   *Universal Issues*

It is chiefly the theses of Bhattacharya's writings that have en-
listed the interest of scholars, critics, and doctoral students East and
West. This does not imply that the author's artistry has been either
overlooked or looked down upon. Rather, it would seem to be recognition of the author's own creative view—not "art for art's sake,"
but art as the conduit for arousing social awareness and concern
that may lead to reform.

Bhattacharya refuses to deal either with surface situations or simple solutions. Circumstances and characters that may at first appear
to be delimited, on closer acquaintance are revealed as components
of a more inclusive spectrum.

Although there are many issues to which Bhattacharya addresses
himself, the major and most inclusive ones seem to me to be those
concerns of today that are universal in nature: individual human
worth and dignity, freedom and national aspiration, and the need
for reconciliation of differences or achievement of equilibrium
among differing views and ways of life, especially between East and

117

West, the traditional and the new. The manifestations of these universal issues and the manner in which they are handled may be peculiarly Indian, immersed in the author's home scene and ethos. This does not, however, invalidate their universality or restrict their appeal; rather, it confirms our human commonality.

II *Human Worth and Dignity*

The dignity and worth of every individual, irrespective of circumstances of birth is affirmed, it seems to me, in every one of the novels. The hunger and deprivation of body and soul, the central concerns of *So Many Hungers!*, may have been occasioned by the juxtaposition of war conditions and widespread drought in Bengal, but the resultant death and devastation spring more basically from the exploitation of the many by the few—from a disregard of the worth of the individual, no matter how destitute or low born.

In *Music for Mohini* the theme is developed in a different way, for this is the first of the novels to center on women characters as moving forces in the action. From this point on, Bhattacharya apparently gives increasing thought to the role of women in contemporary life. Other writers before him were noted for their treatment of the female psyche. But, whereas Flaubert's Emma Bovary, for instance, was a captive of her class and her incurably romantic expectations, to the very end seeking her life force from the men about her, Mohini is the determiner of her own destiny. While Emma is like a captive bird, beating feeble wings against a man-made cage, Mohini is a free spirit whom no cage can hold. Men are essential to her happiness—her father, her husband, the physician Harindra, her young brother, and the boy Ranjan. But, ultimately it is Mohini who shapes their lives, rather than they hers.

All the women in *Music for Mohini* are, in fact, "activists." After our reading is done, they are the ones who live on in the mind most clearly and with a sense of continuing vitality. Though the major theme of the novel undoubtedly is the adjustment of traditional values to new norms, of East to West, a strong accompanying strain is as certainly that of women as determining forces in such adjustment. Bhattacharya—like the late Prime Minister Nehru, philosopher ex-President Sarvepalli Radhakrishnan, and others among India's great leaders—is concerned that as India adapts to a new world it should not be at the sacrifice of human values. In *Music for Mohini* he seems to assert that women are not only among those of worth and dignity, but are at one and the same time strong, active guardians of essential human values and visionary guides to the future.

Actually, "seems to assert" is too weak a statement of the author's purpose, for Bhattacharya himself has said that he believes the women of India have a greater "capacity for value adaptation" than have the men. This is the case, he believes, because the "transition from the old to the new, the crisis of value adaptation strikes deeper into the lives of our women than of our menfolk."[1] In this forthright expression and in his fictional representations Bhattacharya emphasizes the special worth of woman in the social order. More will be said later about women as motivating forces between old and new, East and West.

He Who Rides a Tiger approaches the theme of individual worth by way of attacking the caste system. As in *So Many Hungers!* famine and wartime hardship are the primary anti-social forces. Added to these, however, are what one critic has referred to as "the human cruelty and emotional disfigurement that result from the rigidities of a time-honored system of caste."[2] A dramatic scene mid-way through the story's action reveals the inequities of caste as the central core of Bhattacharya's thesis. Kalo, the humble blacksmith, has by this time lived the life of a Brahmin priest so convincingly that it has become part of him:

He played the Brahminic role with the art of a true Twice-born. *The myth of caste superiority* lay snapped in his hand. Yet he was upholding the same myth, making it his strength. Was it his shield against himself? Or did the sacred thread he wore across his chest gird his inmost soul, too?

One afternoon, as he was strolling in front of the temple, an old destitute man approached him with the cry: "I have not eaten for two days. Will you, sir, give me a few morsels out of your abundance?"

His imploring hand touched the Brahmin's forearm. Baba stepped back quickly. "Rogue!" he shouted in a rage. "How dare you touch me? I shall have to take a bath at this late hour to cleanse myself."

[Lekha] was standing near the gate. She heard, and it seemed to her that a stranger in the image of her father stood before her. "Baba" she cried in pain and protest.

He turned to her. Could he perhaps read her feeling? He had been angered by the touch of a low-caste hand and felt the need for a cleansing bath. . . . Was the smith man gone altogether, leaving no shadow on the Brahminic self?

A quick change showed in his face and manner, as though he were ashamed of himself. The hungry man was walking away down the road. He gave a shout and the man stopped. Kalo strode to him. "Do not mind the sparks of a second's ill-temper, brother. Where is your home?" . . .

Kalo deliberately laid his hand on the stranger's bare shoulder. "*All men are born equal.*" His voice was severe, as if he were settling accounts with himself. "What is your work?" he asked. [Italics mine][3]

When the old man reveals he is a humble *kamar*, a blacksmith, Kalo replies with pride that "there is none better" than he, and takes the man Viswanath as a gardener for the temple grounds. From this point the conscience of Kalo is incarnated in the person of Viswanath.

For centuries caste has been one of India's chief blocks on the road to social reforms that would assure each citizen full stature as a member of the human family. Though "outlawed" in the Constitution adopted following Independence in 1947, caste discrimination is still prevalent, especially in village life. In meeting this "internal" Indian problem head-on and revealing it as a continuing major challenge to the nation's people and leaders, Bhattacharya reveals himself as one of the braver of the literary social critics.

Rabindranath Tagore was one of the earlier of the creative writers to attack the institution of caste. A cathartic cleansing of the temple occurs in his play *Bisarjan* ("Sacrifice"), first performed in 1903. Mulk Raj Anand's novels of social concern also probe the most indigenous of India's communal problems. *Coolie* (1933) and *Untouchable* (1935) both take outcastes as their protagonists and expose the festering sore on the social body that, left untreated, might well endanger the health of a nation struggling to be born. Lesser writers would return to a romanticized past in which caste could either be ignored or viewed as an accepted social convenience; or they would externalize their expressions of protest, directing them chiefly toward colonialists or other foreign influences.

A Goddess Named Gold carries the idea of individual worth and dignity more forcefully into the political arena. The entire thesis of intelligent, informed, and accountable citizenship in a newly democratic society hinges on the idea of self-worth and ethical action. Amulets and other magic formulas must be cast aside, giving way to responsible human endeavor.

Here, as in *Music for Mohini*, women characters are centers of action, though their original strength is somewhat vitiated as the plot unfolds. Meera and her grandmother, so affirmative and forceful at the beginning of the book, lose ground to the unlikely Seth and to the Minstrel, a sort of prime mover *in absentia*. Some readers might have wished that Bhattacharya had realized the early promise of forceful action by the women characters. To be sure, without their intervention, the Seth might well have captured the village's first elective office. On the other hand, Meera's manipulation by both her grandfather (the Minstrel) and the Seth (an alliance that remains difficult for me to accept) delays and even threatens to destroy the birth of democracy in Sonamitti.

Although, as has been implied, the theme of human dignity and worth also runs through *Shadow from Ladakh*, it does not come on as forcefully as in the earlier writings. Here, again, the women characters hold special interest and have special strength. From Suruchi, who opens the action as she returns to India from Moscow, to her daughter Sumita, who closes it after catalyzing the opposing energies of Gandhigram and Steeltown, women hold center stage. All participants in the drama—even the caricatured members of the Lohapur Club and Bhashkar's inimitable personal secretary, Mrs. Mehra—men and women alike, are depicted as having an innate sense of value and worth. Only Satyajit is wracked by doubts, sees himself as less than worthy. Through much of the story he falls short of the standard he has set for himself. But the measure he has used is that of the canonized, "saintly" Gandhiji, rather than fallible man. An essential result of Satyajit's ultimately successful struggle for a resolution of the opposing forces of old and new, tradition and innovation, aggression and preservation, steelmill and spinning wheel, is the realization of his own personhood, his own self-sufficiency. No longer would his worth depend largely upon that of another—even a Gandhi. His victory has been achieved as a result of his own inner strength. Before the shouts of "Victory, victory to Satyajit!" assure him of success on the broader field, he has realized his personal triumph: "He had forced himself into a Gandhian stance and gained victory over himself. And now, if perchance he were to live, he would not have to step on each footprint of the Master's striding gait."[4]

III   *Freedom and National Aspiration*

As has been noted (Chapter 2), Bhattacharya was from his student years in England an active proponent of independence for India.

Freedom and national autonomy form a rich chord running through most of his work and are expressed forcefully or in subtle strains.

One of the more subtle reflections of his national pride I see is in the remarkable absence of non-Indian characters, subjects, and settings in his total writing. There is an innate pride in his consistent reference to the home scene and to the indigenous Indian personality. Furthermore, although giving no sense of regional restriction, Bengal remains the pivot point for setting and action.

Freedom from colonial restraints concerns Bhattacharya, as it did Tagore who so influenced Bhattacharya's life. A more basic concern of both writers, however, is freedom from all debilitating influences, whether from without or within. Nationhood built on the crumbling foundation of outmoded ways and social injustice would be but a facade providing scant shelter for a new state. Like Tagore and Gandhi, Bhattacharya has refused to endorse a chauvinistic platform for India's political life. Even in *Shadow from Ladakh*, regarded by some critics as "self-righteous" and "propagandistic,"[5] it seems to me that his argument for accommodation between China and India, between modernity and traditionalism, between East and West, comes through as the novel's predominating theme. The author finds inner weakness, divisiveness, and lack of vision more threatening to India's position in the contemporary world than any threat from without.

Among the early essays in *Some Memorable Yesterdays* (1941), in which vignettes of great incidents and inspiring figures from India's past are depicted as worthy of continuing pride, introspective analysis also is present. The quotation from Tagore which opens Bhattacharya's portrayal of Ram Mohun Roy, "the Father of Modern India" (1772–1833), lays stress on this point of view, which is shared by Tagore and Bhattacharya:

Ram Mohun Roy . . . was born at a time when our country, having lost its link with the inmost truths of its being, struggled under a crushing load of unreason, in abject slavery to circumstance. In social usage, in politics, in the realm of religion and art, we had entered the zone of uncreative habit, of decadent tradition, and ceased to exercise our humanity. . . ."[6]

It was a failure within, then, as well as the aggression from without, that was the cause for India's colonial subjugation. Without the inner weakness, the outer opposing strength could not have succeeded.

So Many Hungers!, Bhattacharya's bitterest cry against human injustice, was written on the eve of national independence. At the outset, focus is on the war in Europe. The action moves rapidly into the problems that the war foments: deprivation, dislocation, hunger, and exploitation. On the warp of international conflict and national aspiration, the busy shuttle of local village and teeming city carries the threads that weave the whole cloth of everyday life. Bhattacharya is concerned with both warp and weft. Now one strand comes into view, then another. National independence and human dignity, are dependent each upon the unbroken strength of the other. The thread of individual suffering and the strand of national struggle come together symbolically in the story's final scene when Rahoul, being taken across the Ganges Bridge on his way to political imprisonment, sees Kajoli's mother contemplating death in the sacred waters below. "He laughed in his tight-lipped way as he recalled the third freedom. There it was, the freedom from want, even if the four of them, the charter of rights of a hunger-tossed century, did not include the freedom to be free."[7]

Impending nationhood is occasionally mentioned in *Music for Mohini*, but it is not the central theme of the book. As Jayadev returns to the village with his bride he thinks of what meaning life holds for him:

It was his dream to reorientate the values and patterns of Hindu life. India was on the verge of freedom: a new page of world history was writing itself. The political implications were visible to all but not the social problems. What was political liberty worth to the common man if it was not part of a renascence in social life. Jayadev reasoned, as all men of thought reasoned, but his reaction took an altogether individual form. While others borrowed a ready-made sword from Western ideology to cut the knots of the problem, Jayadev delved back into India's remote past for a solution. . . . The purity of ancient thought had been lost in misinterpretation until the dignity of man had become a mere plaything of vested interest. Jayadev would break the crust of vulgarity and reveal ancient thought in its true splendor. But the new man of his vision, growing to his full stature, was not to be a hollow reincarnation, not a spiritless copy of ancient Hindu man. That were as stupid as a Hindu moulded in a Western pattern. . . .

So Jayadev was possessed by his dream of true freedom. . . . Look back that you may look forward. Look to the roots of India in this fateful hour of flowering. Use the buried material of the past to write the new social charter.[8]

For Jayadev, then, freedom resides in the Golden Age of the ancient Vedic period. Though he dreams here of freedom of individual
and nation, it is a freedom bound to the past. For months Mohini
will struggle to become the living prototype of Maitreyi, the ideal
Vedic woman—self-assured, with keenly honed intellect. The mold
is not Mohini's however, and one of the notes in the theme of freedom in *Music for Mohini* is the discordant one of Jayadev's efforts
to reincarnate Maitreya in Mohini's form. Individual freedom, especially from the dead hand of the past, is of paramount importance
in the life of Mohini and in her story.

It is only with the entrance of Harindra, the young physician
educated in Western medicine, late in the action, that Jayadev is
brought to the reluctant recognition that thought alone cannot effect
the transformation he desires; it must be wedded to action. Harindra's struggle against outmoded medical practices becomes part of
the larger struggle against a stultifying past and part of the battle
for freedom on all fronts—a freedom that must lead ultimately to
an autonomous India whose problems will be her opportunities. Jayadev sees the survival of the Big House—the ancestral home and
influence—as dependent upon creative participation in India's new
world:

> The battle for economic freedom . . . was in full swing and ten years
> hence there would be no landed gentry to live on the peasantry. India was
> fast moving that way. But then, would the people, fed well, be free in spirit
> because of their new physical state? The answer was plain. It was the crux
> of India's problem.
>
> It was the test and crisis, too, of the Big House. Would the Big House
> topple into oblivion with a hundred others like it? . . . Even when it crum-
> bled to dust, as it must, the Big House could live by progressive leadership.[9]

He Who Rides a Tiger brings together in one thread the filaments
of three basic freedoms—freedom from want, from stultifying tradition (especially in caste and religion), and from foreign rule. As
a strong thread depends upon the contributing tension of all its
fibres, so the social health of a people depends upon the assurance
of its basic freedoms. At the conclusion of his struggles against the
forces of poverty and lowly birth, Kalo repudiates the duplicity of
his action, but not the action itself. Assuming the guise of a Brahmin
priest, he has saved himself and his daughter from destitution. In
publicly revealing his charade, he has revealed the absurdity of caste

distinction. Finally, in supporting Viswanath's diversion of the temple's "holy milk" to the starving children of the community, he has asserted his individual responsibility for the well-being of his fellows. From Biten, who has renounced the Brahminic status, comes praise of Kalo's courageous final acts—praise that echoes the song of freedom toward which an enlightened and responsible people progresses:

"You have chosen, my friend. You have triumphed over those others—and over yourself. What you have done just now will steel the spirit of hundreds and thousands of us. Your story will be a legend of freedom, a legend to inspire and awaken.[10]

As has been emphasized in the earlier discussion of *A Goddess Named Gold* (Chapter 6), the core of this fourth Bhattacharya novel is the achievement of nationhood. The problems with which India struggled as she faced the dawn of a new way of life are the problems many other re-emerging nations have faced in the intervening quarter of a century, and which are confronting still others about to be born. Through skillful use of the devices of fiction, Bhattacharya probes the responsibilities of citizen action in a democratic nation just emerging from centuries of foreign domination. Characterization, situation, and action—honest tools of the novelist's craft—all offer responses. And these responses are harmonized in an antiphony between the Minstrel grandfather and the villagers of Sonamitti in the novel's concluding scene:

"Speak, son." The minstrel gave the stranger [Sohanlal] an encouraging nod and was then startled to hear him cry, "We will not let the wanderer go. We will make him stay with us. That will be his best gift to us, to the village."

A burst of approval. "You cannot leave us, minstrel-brother."

"That is not all we ask," Sohanlal continued. "He will have to use his wisdom for Sonamitti, and what is the best way to force his hand?"

"Tell us."

He answered in a big shout, "Vote for our minstrel-brother, vote!"

An astonished pause, and then the thunderous cry, "Vote for our minstrel-brother, vote!" . . .

The minstrel was taken aback. "That is not right," a distressed murmur. . . .

"You cannot deny us. This is the demand of one and all."

"No, no." His agitation grew visibly. "The board is no place for a minstrel. . . ."

The answer came:

"Brother, you will make those men share your faith in the future."

"You will release them from a past now dead and gone."

"You talk of a house to be built. Will you shirk the task of laying the first few bricks?"

And with hope and love and jubilation the people cried, "Vote for our minstrel-brother, vote!" . . .

He cried, "Friends, I am a wandering man. You cannot tie me down. You must not." He shook his head vehemently.

Then Meera spoke.

"Grandpapa—" Her voice was husky. "Look at us, look at the village. What you seek in your long wandering is here before you. Then why do you want to leave us again? . . ."

"Pray, listen—" The minstrel tried again, but the conviction faltered within him as he spoke and the ring of his words was hollow."[11]

So, the wisest minds—minds grounded in the verities of the past—and visionary eyes, eyes that are not blinded to the future—must be called into public office. Having been wooed by the charlatanry of the Seth and tempted by the seemingly easy path to prosperity offered by Meera's magic *taveez*, with the leadership of the enlightened mind of the educated Sohanlal (who recognized the ending of an age and the village's "tryst with destiny"), the unlettered villagers of Sonamitti walk into the future, assuming the responsibilities as well as the privileges of the hard-won freedom.

Returning for a moment to the important role played by women in Bhattacharya's writing, a striking aspect of *A Goddess Named Gold* is the leadership taken by the women of Sonamitti in the march toward nationhood. From the opening of the action, it is the women of the village who are alert to the changes that freedom and autonomy will mean to India and to their small segment of the nation. They recall the glory of their participation in the freedom movement:

"Those days—Sohagi, remember? Gandhi-ji touched our spirit as it slept. Wakened, we became the equals of our menfolk. Proud, chins up, we marched in a column of our own, across the meadow to Pipli, onward to Kanhan. 'Quit India!' we shouted to the Engrez aliens in one big voice."

"We were all afire," Sohagi said . . . "Wherever we went, women came flocking out of field, barn and kitchen to cry with us 'Quit!' "[12]

But new challenges require renewed determination and new struggle in which the women see themselves not only as active participants, but quite appropriately as leaders. Dr. Marlene Fisher in her article, "The Women in Bhattacharya's Novels,"[13] points out that, despite their seeming submissiveness, women have traditionally played active and formative roles in Indian society. In recent history, they were side by side with their men in the freedom protest demonstrations that preceded Independence, as Bhattacharya has depicted above. "Their numbers and courage," Dr. Fisher writes, "both equally noticeable, helped burst the walls of the pre-1947 prisons in which they were confined alongside their husbands, fathers, brothers."

Freedom is surely the tocsin in *Shadow from Ladakh*—freedom from aggression, freedom from myopic adherence to the past, and freedom from domination by the alien influences in India today. The future must be an amalgam of old and new, a balance between indigenous and alien (largely Western mechanization), an agreement between neighboring peoples.

Across the vale of Ladakh in 1967 the two re-awakened giants of Asia, both in the pride of their nationhood, threatened world conflagration. What happens when the affirmative values of national aspiration are thrown into the steaming cauldron of international rivalry and opposed loyalties? What happens to the cherished freedoms of the individual Indian, the individual Chinese?

Bhattacharya's answer is given through the action at the village level where the conflict between China and India is paralleled and made immediate by the conflict between Steeltown and Gandhigram. The antagonism between governments, like that between opposing ways of life, Bhattacharya sees as being worked out ultimately in terms of their human components—the living entities that make up the seeming monoliths that are State and Society. Time and again, through character and plot, Bhattacharya makes the dual meaning clear. One of the more overt instances is when Bhashkar, sitting with his newly acquired Chinese "daughters," listens to Prime Minister Nehru speaking on the radio urging his people not to think of the Chinese people with "anger and bitterness" because of the present quarrel between governments.

Points of view, loyalties, that may seem at first unalterably opposed need not remain so. The answer lies in the ability of every human being to open his mind to new ideas and to turn his face toward the winds of change. Thus differing views can coalesce, and new life patterns can merge with and enrich the old.

IV   *Reconciliation and Equilibrium*

The conclusion of the action in *Shadow from Ladakh* forcefully
expresses reconciliation of oppositions, the third major strain that
runs through Bhattacharya's novels, as well as many of his essays
and public addresses.

After the steel workers of Lohapur have expressed their admira-
tion for Satyajit's soul struggle in support of the old values by
marching toward Gandhigram (a symbolic "return to the roots"),
the once hard and aggressive Bhashkar recognizes the way in which
a union of values has taken place within himself; recognizes Sumita
as the personification of this union:

> Bhashkar stared into the night. There lay the village that had forced upon
> him a revision of his mental attitudes. Satyajit had had his share. And Suruchi.
> But more than either—Sumita. She went away, but the power that she was
> remained.
>
> He recalled his first impression of Sumita. He had not liked her. The
> coarse white garb, the eyes too big and calm. She was far from his idea of
> an attractive woman. And later, when he had known her at close range, he
> had felt repelled by his glimpse of the father image.
>
> Strange, then, that she became a fixation in his mind! He could not have
> believed that such a thing might happen. It happened against his conscious
> will. When she went away, even in his utter forlornness he felt a kind of
> relief; relief at the thought that none of his values would have to be changed.
>
> But deep within him Sumita was still supreme. And revolt was futile. . . .[14]

The theme of the need for amalgamation of differing ways is the
strongest of the strains running through *Music for Mohini*, as has
been said earlier. Mohini's relatively emancipated and free life in
the city—with her radio career, the Western movies, the study in
co-educational classes—stands at the opposite pole from Jayadev's
village and the Big House. Though Jayadev recognizes the inequities
built into the traditional ways, until Mohini's life begins to affect
his own, he seeks solutions largely through learning rather than in
action. As she speaks to Mohini of Jayadev's seeking "in ancient
thought sanction for the West-influenced ideals"[15] of the time,
Roop-lekha captures a sense of the visionary mind too immersed
in its idealistic musings to move into action.

It is Roop-lekha, Jayadev's sister, and Mohini, his wife, who come
to be the living strands binding the oppositions of old and new, East
and West. Entering the confusing complexity of the city as a sixteen-

year-old bride, Roop-lekha had brought with her the teachings of Mother and the traditions of the Big House. Significantly, it is she who is instrumental in finding Mohini for her brother. As a result of Roop-lekha's intervention, then, Mohini later carries the values of the city back to the village. So the shuttle has been set in motion that will help to weave the fabric that is the new India—a whole cloth, in which the richness of the past is intermingled with the iridescence of today.

As Mohini prepares to leave Behula to return home for the first time since her marriage, she is content with the harmony that has now been effected in her life: "At last there was no discord. Life was music . . ."[16] The implication is that harmony has been achieved on the broader scale of the nation itself.

In *A Goddess Named Gold* Bhattacharya brings to center stage the need for reconciliation or equilibrium between contending forces within the individual and society—a heightened need as India stands on the brink of nationhood and prepares for her first popular elections. If the new nation is to survive, every citizen must assume his share of responsibility in accordance with his personal endowments. Every segment of society must also recognize and fulfill its role. Youth and old age, as epitomized by Meera and her grandfather; old and new, East and West, village and city, summed up in the personalities of the simple villagers and Sohanlal, the educated young city man—all these must meet, reconcile their differences, and be brought into balance if the new government is to go forward into the future with strength.

This thesis, as well as the more obvious one of freedom and national aspiration, concerns every self-governed people, and especially those just emerging from centuries of rule by foreign powers. Without the inner unity that comes from the reconciliation of divisive forces and the establishment of equilibrium in the life of a people, a new government begins from a base of weakness.

The conclusion of the action in *A Goddess Named Gold* makes clear the message of individual responsibility in meeting a new age. The Seth's efforts to manipulate the villagers to gain their votes for the "board-moard" and to turn Meera's magic amulet to his own profit have been exposed and aborted. At the other end of the spectrum, the Minstrel, revered almost as a saint, has been forced to go beyond preachment to practice. No longer will he be able to withdraw from reality by wandering the countryside singing the ancient lays extolling the golden age of India's former glory. "Brothers, now that we have freedom, we need acts of faith," he has told the people of Sonamitti. Their reply is to demand of him his own "act of faith" by representing the village on the district board. Had not he, himself, pointed out to Meera, when the Seth first tried to manipulate the villagers for his own purposes, that "the wheels of life would run henceforth under the power of the people's vote" and, realizing that, did they want to send this "tyrant" to the district board to "speak and act" for them?[17] The reply comes from the people, inspired by the enlightened Sohanlal, that the Minstrel himself is the one best suited to represent them. About the figure of this man of wisdom and probity have coalesced the diverse factions of the village. Differences resolved, the people have taken their first step into the nation's future.

In *He Who Rides A Tiger* the concept of reconciliation of differences is worked out mainly through the character of Kalo, as are the book's other themes. At the conclusion of the traumatic experiences that have marked his journey from village to city, from low caste to high, from self-acceptance to self-knowledge, Kalo has reconciled the bitter divisions that had once rent his personality. He and Chandra Lekha are once more truly united—not as partners in a cruel charade of duplicity, but as father and daughter facing life together honestly and with dignity. Bhattacharya does not detail for us what that future will bring but he has hinted at marriage between Lekha and Biten—a wedding between the confined village and the wider world, between ancient ways and new—and he has indicated that Viswanath—the personification of Kalo's conscience—will have a part in it.

Among the strands running through the plot of *So Many Hungers!* is that dealing with the increasing involvement of Rahoul and Monju in the social and political issues of the day. The husband and wife, who at the outset of the action are preoccupied by the birth of their daughter and for whom the news of world conflict is not much more than disembodied radio reports, by the conclusion of the story are devoting themselves to the welfare of the starving masses, while Rahoul faces imprisonment for his leadership in the nationalist movement. Yet, in a denouement that might well have remained steeped in recrimination, the author makes room for one of his deepest convictions. Even in the impassioned speech in which Rahoul calls for the colonial government to withdraw from India, there is the balancing note that acknowledges the affirmative values of the British presence.

"Quit India!" cried the two million dead of Bengal. The anger was warm in his voice, and he paused till his speech was cool again. "Quit!" cried all India. *"You have done us some good* along with much evil. *For the good you've done* you have been paid in full. The accounts have been settled. Now, for God's sake, quit!" [Italics mine][18]

And, at the very end, as his captors take Rahoul away, "his mind was without hate, without anger, in a *nirvana* of passionlessness.[19]

This, it seems to me, sums up the Bhattacharya attitude. Great and just causes should—and will—totally engage the men and women dedicated to those causes. But only when hate and anger are surmounted and the contestants enter "a *nirvana* of passionlessness" will lasting and valid resolutions be reached. In exposing the injustices and hardships that have plagued his people in recent years, Bhattacharya has eschewed easy solutions. There are none. And there will be no easy solutions in an increasingly complex future.

In his essay "The Nature of Wisdom"[20] (see Chapter 8) Bhattacharya presents the teachings of the ancient and revered *Bhagavad Gita* as the light for today and tomorrow. He writes there:

What gives the *Gita* its own individuality is its strong insistence on the establishment of a dynamic equilibrium in the art of living. That equilibrium is essential in both intrapersonal and interpersonal relationships, and is the way to self-fulfilment.

As "dynamic equilibrium" is necessary in inner life and the immediate "interpersonal" surroundings, so it is necessary on the broader world scale. The "enemy of the darkness of the farther road" may well be found in the verities of the *Gita*, and the verities of the *Gita*, it seems to me, help to form the bedrock on which the structure of Bhattacharya's fiction has been built.

Notes and References

Chapter One

1. Michael Edwardes, *British India: 1772–1947* (New York: Taplinger Publishing Company, 1968), p. 119.
2. *Ibid.*, p. 133.
3. *Ibid.*, pp. 176–77.
4. Quoted from *Impact! Asian Views of the West*, edited by JoAnn White (New York: Simon & Schuster, 1971), pp. 183–84.
5. Nayantara Sahgal, "From Fear Set Free," *Impact!*, pp. 109, 113.

Chapter Two

1. The autobiographical passages quoted throughout this chapter are from informal reminiscences jotted down for me by Bhattacharya in Honolulu, February 1972.
2. "Criminal Investigation Department." Of the C.I.D. purposes and activity Bhattarcharya has written (January 1974): "A political police force established early in this century to combat anti-British movements. Even Tagore was under their constant investigation—the Poet has recorded that, and mentioned censorship of his mail."
3. Unless otherwise indicated, quotations in this section are from a conversation with Dr. and Mrs. Bhattacharya in Honolulu in 1971.
4. Writing from St. Louis, Missouri, January, 1974.
5. *The Age*, Melbourne, March 28, 1962.
6. Letter from Bhattacharya, July 22, 1973.
7. Letter, January 31, 1974.

Chapter Three

1. Page references are to Jaico Books pocket edition (Bombay: Jaico Publishing House, 1964).
2. In a personal interview with me in Honolulu, 1972.

Chapter Four

1. Page references are to Jaico Books pocket edition (Bombay: Jaico Publishing House, 1964).
2. Conversation in Honolulu, 1971.

133

Chapter Five

1. Page references are to Hind Pocket Books edition (New Delhi: Indra-prastha Press, 1955).
2. Professor Edwin Gerow, University of Chicago, 1973.
3. Bhattacharya himself dismisses the Hitrec comment, saying he does not understand what Hitrec is getting at. And Millen Brand, Bhattacharya's editor at Crown Publishers, finds the comment "condescending and untrue." In his letter to me of August 22, 1973, Brand wrote: "I never had any awareness of [Bhattacharya's] 'trying to free himself' from the quality of incantation, whatever that may be. The cadence of villagers' speech, I always assumed was there in life, and this is the only incantatory element I'm aware of."

Chapter Six

1. Page references are to the Hind Pocket Books edition (Delhi: Hind Pocket Books Ltd., 1968).
2. Mary K. Sweeny in *America*, October 8, 1960.
3. Percy Wood in *The Chicago Tribune*, September 25, 1960.
4. Letter to me, August 22, 1973.
5. Review entitled "A Parable Set in India," ca. 1960. Periodical unknown.

Chapter Seven

1. Page references are to the Hind Pocket Book edition (Delhi: Hind Pocket Books Ltd., 1966).
2. *Gandhi the Writer* (New Delhi: National Book Trust, India, October 2, 1969), p. 97.
3. Interview with Bhattacharya, 1972.
4. Letter to me, September 24, 1973.
5. Wm. Theodore de Bary, *et al.*, *Sources of Indian Tradition* (New York: Columbia University Press, 1964), Vol. I, p. 276.
6. Sarah Ensley Brandel, *Literature East & West* (Vol. XI, No. 2, June 1967), p. 210.
7. Patricia L. Sharpe, *Mahfil: A Quarterly of South Asian Literature* (Vol. V, Nos. 1 & 2, 1968–69), p. 135.
8. *Mahfil* (Vol. V, Nos. 1 & 2), pp. 44–45.
9. Letter to Crown Publishers, July 5, 1966.
10. *Mahfil* (Vol. V, Nos. 1 & 2), p. 134.
11. *Literature East & West* (Vol. XI, No. 2, June 1967), pp. 209–10.

Chapter Eight

1. *The Aryan Path* (Bombay: Theosophy Co., September 1955), pp. 392–96.

2. Bidyut Sarker, editor, *India and Southeast Asia: Proceedings of Seminar on India and Southeast Asia* (New Delhi: Indian Council for Cultural Relations, 1968), pp. 99–101.

3. Presented at a conference held on the occasion of the inauguration of Dr. Harlan Cleveland as President of the University of Hawaii, March 17, 1970. At that time Bhattacharya was a Senior Specialist in the East-West Center, Honolulu.

4. *Abbottempo* (North Chicago: Abbott Laboratories, 1971, Book I), pp. 2–4.

5. *Rabindranath Tagore, 1861–1961: A Centenary Volume* (New Delhi: Sahitya Akademi, November 1961), pp. 96–101.

6. In the Centenary Volume Bhattacharya joined a galaxy of world figures in paying homage to one of the most creatively productive geniuses in human history. Some of the writers and their theses: Mulk Raj Anand, "Tagore, Reconciler of East and West"; Buddhadeva Bose, "Rabindranath Tagore and Bengali Prose"; Pearl Buck, "A World Poet"; Umashankar Joshi, "Tagore's Poetic Vision"; Toshihiko Katayama, "A Homage to Tagore from Japan"; Albert Schweitzer, "Tagore, the Goethe of India"; Robert Frost, "Tagore's Poetry Overflowed National Boundaries"; Sonakul Dhani, "Tagore's Visit to Siam"; Halldor Laxness, "Gitanjali in Iceland"; Nguyen-Dang-Thuc, "Tagore and Vietnam."

7. *The Statesman* (New Delhi: May 1968).

8. All page references are to *Indian Cavalcade* (Bombay: Nalanda Publications, May 1948).

9. *Steel Hawk and Other Stories* (Delhi: Hind Pocket Books Ltd., 1968), p. 112.

Chapter Nine

1. This and other quotations in this section are from a conversation in Honolulu, June 1971.

2. *The Golden Boat* (Bombay: Jaico Publishing House, third edition, May 1964), p. 5. (All page references are to this edition.)

3. Page references are to *Gandhi the Writer: The Image As It Grew* (New Delhi: National Book Trust, India, October 2, 1969).

4. *A Goddess Named Gold* (Delhi: Hind Pocket Books Ltd., 2nd impression, August 1967), p. 303.

5. *Shadow from Ladakh* (Delhi: Hind Pocket Books Ltd., 1966), p. 70.

6. *Ibid.*, pp. 104–105.

7. *Ibid.*, p. 339.

Chapter Ten

1. In a talk, "Women in My Stories," given in October 1973, at the University of Washington, Seattle.

2. Marlene Fisher, "Personal and Social Change in Bhattacharya's Novels," *World Literature Written in English* (Vol. 12, No. 2, November 1973), p. 293.

3. *He Who Rides a Tiger*, pp. 109–10.

4. *Shadow from Ladakh*, pp. 352–53.

5. Patricia L. Sharpe in her review (*Mahfil: A Quarterly of South Asian Literature*, Vol. V., Nos. 1 & 2, 1968–69, pp. 134–39) speaks of the Sahitya Akademi Award as having been made on the basis of the "propaganda" value of *Shadow from Ladakh*, saying, "Reading it probably made officialdom feel very good."

6. *Indian Cavalcade* (*Some Memorable Yesterdays*), p. 200.

7. *So Many Hungers!*, p. 214.

8. *Music for Mohini*, pp. 79–80.

9. *Ibid.*, p. 170.

10. *He Who Rides a Tiger*, p. 232.

11. *A Goddess Named Gold*, pp. 305–306.

12. *Ibid.*, p. 6.

13. *World Literature Written in English* (Vol. 11, No. 1, April 1972), pp. 95–108.

14. *Shadow from Ladakh*, p. 357.

15. *Music for Mohini*, p. 114.

16. *Ibid.*, p. 232.

17. *A Goddess Named Gold*, p. 70.

18. *So Many Hungers!*, p. 212.

19. *Ibid.*, p. 214.

20. *Abbottempo*.

Selected Bibliography

PRIMARY SOURCES

I. *Works in the Original*

"After Vietnam, What?" Unpublished paper read at conference, University of Hawaii, March 17, 1970.

"Baseless Prejudice Against Indians Writing English." Article in *The Statesman*, New Delhi, Aug. 1968.

"Bridge Between the Peoples, A." An essay in *India and Southeast Asia: Proceedings of a Seminar*. New Delhi: Indian Council for Cultural Relations, 1968, pp. 99–101.

"Cartman and the Steel Hawk, The." Short story in *An Adventure in Asian and Australian Writing: Span*, Lionel Wigmore, ed. Melbourne: F. W. Cheshire, 1958.

"City of Cities is Now Called Callous." Article in *India: A Survey Compiled from the Times*. London: Times Publishing Co., 1962.

Contemporary Indian Short Stories, Series II. Edited by Bhabani Bhattacharya. New Delhi: Sahitya Akademi, 1967.

"Crocodile Pool, The." Short story in *The Countryman*. Oxford, 1950.

"Europe—Behind the Veil." Series of articles in *The Hindu*, Madras, 1930.

"Faltering Pendulum, The." Short story in *Life & Letters*, London, Vol. 65, No. 152, April 1950, pp. 43–48.

Gandhi the Writer: The Image As It Grew. A literary biography. New Delhi: National Book Trust, 1969.

Goddess Named Gold, A. Fourth Novel. New York: Crown Publishers, 1960; Delhi: Hind Pocket Books, 1967.

Golden Boat, The. Translations from Rabindranath Tagore. London: *The Spectator*, 1929; Allen & Unwin, 1930; New York: Macmillan, 1930; Bombay: Jaico Publishing House, 1955.

"Hawkers in an Indian Noon." Sketch in *Asia* magazine. New York, 1935.

He Who Rides a Tiger. Third novel. New York: Crown Publishers, 1954; Bombay: Jaico Publishing House, 1955; London: Angus and Robertson, 1960; Delhi: Hind Pocket Books, 1955, 1973.

"Hollow Arbiters of the Writer's Destiny." Article criticizing literary critics. *The Statesman*, New Delhi, May 1968.

"How I Wrote *So Many Hungers!*" Article in *Letteraturnaya Gazetta*, Moscow, 1951.

"In London Today." Biweekly feature in *The Hindu*. Madras, 1930.

Indian Cavalcade (Some Memorable Yesterdays). Sketches from *The Hindu*, *Mysindia*, and *The Aryan Path*. Bombay: Nalanda Publications, 1948.

"Lattu Ram Has an Adventure." Sketch in *The Spectator*. London, 1930.

"Lifelong Dynamism." Article on Tagore, in *Hemisphere*. Sydney, 1961.

"Literature and Social Reality." Article in *The Aryan Path*. Bombay, Sept. 1955, pp. 392–96.

"Maghna Calls, Maghna, The." Short story in *The Aryan Path*. Bombay, 1939.

"Mere Monkeys." Short story in *The Countryman*. Oxford, 1954.

"Moment of Eternity, A." Short story in anthology, *Contemporary Indian Short Stories*. New Delhi: Sahitya Akademi, 1959.

Music for Mohini. Second novel. Serialized in *The Illustrated Weekly*, Bombay, 1950; New York: Crown Publishers, 1952; London: Angus & Robertson, 1959; Bombay: Jaico Publishing House, 1964.

"Nature of Wisdom, The." Essay in *Abbottempo* (international magazine published in English, French, German, Dutch, Spanish, Greek, Turkish, Japanese). North Chicago: Abbott Universal Ltd., 1970.

One Hundred and One Poems by Rabindranath Tagore. Bombay: Asia Publishing House, 1966. Includes Bhattacharya translations, pp. 62–68, 88, 89.

"People of the Villages Change Their Theme, The." Article in *The Times*. London, Jan. 23, 1961.

"Pilgrims in Uniform." Short story in *The Aryan Path*. Bombay, 1939.

Shadow from Ladakh. Fifth novel. New York: Crown Publishers, 1966; London: W. H. Allen, 1967; Delhi: Hind Pocket Books, 1968.

So Many Hungers! First novel. Bombay: Hind Kitabs, 1947; London: Victor Gollancz, 1947; Bombay: Jaico Publishing House, 1964.

Some Memorable Yesterdays. Selections from *The Hindu* weekly feature articles. Patna: Pustak Bhandar, 1941.

"Speed." Sketch in *The Manchester Guardian*, 1929; *The Christian Science Monitor*, Boston, 1930.

Steel Hawk and Other Stories. Delhi: Hind Pocket Books, 1968.

"Tagore as a Novelist." Essay in *Rabindranath Tagore, 1861–1961: A Centenary Volume*. New Delhi: Sahitya Akademi, 1961, pp. 96–101.

"This Week in History." Weekly feature in *The Hindu*, Madras, 1935–36.

Towards Universal Man. Essays by Rabindranath Tagore, selected and edited by Bhabani Bhattacharya, under the auspices of the Tagore Commemorative Volume Society. Bombay: Asia Publishing House, 1961.

II. *Translations of Novels and Short Stories (selected)*

"Affen." German translation by Erica Kalmer of the short story "Mere Monkeys." Hamburg: *Die Welt*. Aug. 12, 1952; Zurich: *Schweizer Familien-Wochenblatt*, Dec. 4, 1952; Zurich: *Volksrecht*, No. 105, 1953;

Linz: *Oberösterreichische Nachrichten.* March 20, 1954; Nurnberg: *Nürnberger Nachrichten,* Nov. 15, 1963; Mannheim: *Mannheimer Morgen,* Feb. 22, 1964; Köln: *Welt der Arbeit,* Nov. 12, 1965; Vienna: *Weiner Zeitung,* Nov. 30, 1963.

Aki Tigrisen Lovagol. Hungarian translation by Szijgyarto Laszlo of *He Who Rides a Tiger.* Budapest: Kossuth Konyvkiado, 1964.

Alle Warten auf das Wunder. German translation of *A Goddess Named Gold.* Frankfurt: Horst Erdmann Verlag, 1962.

"Bar Jedes Menschlichen Gefuhls." German translation by Erica Kalmer of the short story "No Human Feelings." Vienna: *Arbeiter-Zeitung,* Feb. 25, 1951.

Bevrijdend Bedrog. Dutch translation of *He Who Rides a Tiger.* Antwerp: N. V. Standaard Boekhandel, 195(?).

"Crocodile Pool, The." Short story in *Ogonizok* magazine, Moscow, 1953; in Polish anthology, *Adjanta,* Warsaw, 1956; and in *Following the Sun: Seventeen Tales from Australia, India, South Africa.* Berlin: Seven Seas Publishers, 1960.

Czlowick ktory Jedzie Na Tygrysie. Polish translation of *He Who Rides a Tiger.* Warsaw: Czytelnik, 1955.

Das Spiel mit dem Tampel. German translation of *He Who Rides a Tiger.* Berlin: Verlag Volk und Welt, 1958.

De Wereld Wacht Een Wonder. Dutch translation of *A Goddess Named Gold.* Den Haag: Ad. M. C. Stok, n.d.

Den Som Rider Pd En Tiger. Danish translation of *He Who Rides a Tiger.* Copenhagen: Schonberg, 1956.

"Der Aufstand der Frauen." German translation by Erica Kalmer of the short story "Women in Revolt." Buenos Aires: *Argentinisches Tagblatt,* Feb. 25, 1951; Basle: *National Zeitung,* August 9, 1953; Cologne: *Welt der Arbeit,* No. 44, 1950; Stuttgart: *Druck und Papier,* June 1, 1956; Vienna: *Die Presse,* March 14, 1964; Bern: *Berner Tagblatt,* Sept. 25, 1965; Mannheim: *Mannheimer Morgen,* July 1, 1964; Zurich: *Volksrecht,* Feb. 22, 1965; Vienna: *Die Frau,* No. 37, 1966.

"Der Krokodilpfuhl." German translation by Erica Kalmer of the short story "The Crocodile Pool." Buenos Aires: *Argentinsches Tagblatt,* Nov. 29, 1953; Klagenfurt: *Die Neue Zeit,* Nov. 1, 1953; Vienna: *Neues Osterreich,* June 30, 1957.

"Der Quacksalber." German translation by Erica Kalmer of the short story "The Quack." Vienna: *Neues Osterreich,* Oct. 22, 1966; Basle: *Basler Nachrichten,* March 6, 1966; Wetzlar: *Wetzlarer Neue Zeitung,* March 1, 1968.

"Die Akrobaten." German translation by Erica Kalmer of the short story "The Acrobats." Zurich: *Mosaik,* Feb. 2, 1968; Cologne: *Chic,* Dec. 1967; Vienna: *Die Presse,* Sept. 7, 1968; Bremen: *Bremer Nachrichten,* Jan. 4, 1969; Braunschweig: *Braunschweiger Zeitung,* March 30, 1969;

Aachen: *Krichenzeitung*, May 31, 1970; Vienna: *RZ Illustrierte Roman-zeitung*, April 25, 1971.

Dreiging uit Ladakh. Dutch translation of *Shadow from Ladakh*. Den Haag: Ad. M. C. Stok, 1969.

"Ein Autobus Namens Sankhini." German translation by Erica Kalmer of the short story "A Bus Named Sankhini." Zurich: *Volksrecht*, Sept. 9, 1950; Hamburg: *Die Welt*, July 8, 1950; Munich: *Neue Zeitung*, Nov. 14, 1950; Vienna: *Die Presse*, March 22, 1953; Klagenfurt: *Die Neue Zeit*, June 5, 1954; Bern: *Berner Tagblatt*, July 27, 1956; Mannheim: *Mann-heimer Morgen*, Jan. 28, 1955.

"Ein Merkwurdiger Martyrer." German translation by Erica Kalmer of the short story "Pictures in the Fire." Munich: *Die Neue Zeitung*, May 22, 1950; Hamburg: *Die Welt*, Sept. 2, 1950; Buenos Aires: *Argentinisches Tagblatt*, April 29, 1951; Basle: *Basler Nachrichten*, April 21, 1951; Winterthur: *Winterthurer Tagblatt*, Sept. 11, 1956.

"Ein Paar Zufälle." German translation by Erica Kalmer of the sketch "Just Coincidence?" Vienna: *Wiener Zeitung*, July 21, 1966; Oldenburg: *Nordwest Zeitung*, July 19, 1967; St. Gallen: *St. Gallen Tagblatt*, Jan. 14, 1970.

El Que Cabalga un Tigre. Spanish translation by Miguel Angel Asturias of *He Who Rides a Tiger*. Buenos Aires: Goyanarte, 1958.

El'iot Hazahav. Hebrew translation by Targumah Ruth Cohen of *A Goddess Named Gold*. Tel-Aviv: Amihai-Y. Orlinsky, 1964.

"Feigen." German translation by Erica Kalmer of the short story "A Palmful of Figs." Anthologized in *Der sprechende Pflug*. Frankfurt: Erdmann Verlag, 1962. Also, Zurich: *Volksrecht*, April 17, 1950; Basle: *National-Zeitung*, March 26, 1950; Vienna: *Wiener Bilderwoche*, March 9, 1950; Hamburg: *Die Welt*, April 6, 1950; Cologne: *Welt der Arbeit*, April 10, 1953; Koblenz: *Rhein-Zeitung*, March 22, 1953; Essen: *Neue Ruhr-Zeitung*, May 6, 1953; Stade: *Stader Tagblatt*, Jan. 17, 1954; Vienna: *Neues Osterreich*, March 20, 1955; Freiburg: *Badische Zeitung*, June 4, 1955; Graz: *Neue Zeit*, April 1, 1956; Dortmund: *Westfälische Rund-schau*, June 1, 1955; Augsburg: *Frau im Leben*, March 1972; Vienna: *Die Frau*, Aug. 5, 1972; Zurich: *Mosaik*, No. 31, 1972.

Foamente în Bengal. Romanian translation by Petre Solomon of *So Many Hungers*! Bucharest: Editura de Stat Pentru Literatura si Arta, 1956.

Goddess Named Gold, A. German translation (quarterly book club selection). Frankfurt: Erdmann Verlag, 1962.

Golod. Russian translation of *So Many Hungers!* Moscow: Izdat Inostrannoi Litoraturi, 1949.

He Who Rides a Tiger. French, 1956; Serbo-Croatian (Yugoslav), German, Finnish, Sinhalese, and Spanish, 1957; Slovak, Chinese, East German, Hindi, Telegu, and Malayalam, 1958; Czech, 1959; Urdu by Razya Zaheer,

New Delhi: Jamia Malia, 1960; Kannada, Mysore: Kavyalaya Publishers, 1960.

HE WHO RIDES A TIGER. Translations into Russian languages: by I. Bajshnoras, Vilnius: State Lit. Pub., 1960; by O. Krugerskaya & F. Lur'e, Moscow: Izd-vo Inostr. lit., 1956; into Moldavian by E. David, Kishenev: Kartja moldobenjaske, 1960; into Tadzhik by Zh. Ikrami, Dushanbe: Tadzhikoizat, 1958; into Ukrainian, Kiev: Goslitizdat USSR, 1959; from Urdu into Uzbek by N. Muxamedov; Tashkent: Izd-vo Lit. i iskus. im. G. Guljam, 1972.

Hlad Se Vali Do Indie. Czech translation of *So Many Hungers!* Prague: Nakladatelstvi Prace, 1950.

Hunger Och langtan. Swedish translation of *So Many Hungers!* Stockholm: Folket i Bildis Förlag, 1953.

"Im Schatten des Saturns." German translation by Erica Kalmer of the short story "The Baleful Planet." Hanover: *Hannoversche Presse*, Dec. 31, 1965; Vienna: *Neues Osterreich*, Aug. 7, 1965; Zurich: *Elle*, No. 13, 1966; Wuppertal: *General-Anzeiger*, March 8, 1969; Vienna: *RZ Illustrierte Romanzeitung*, Dec. 7, 1969; Bern: *Berner Tagblatt*, April 4, 1970.

"In Den Hohlen von Ajanta." German translation by Erica Kalmer of the short story "She Born of Light." Vienna: *Die Presse*, Oct. 18, 1969.

"Indian Cinema, The." Biweekly feature articles in *The Statesman*, Calcutta, 1935.

Kajoli. German translation of *So Many Hungers!* Berlin: Aufbau Verlag, 1954.

Kdo Jede Na Tygru. Czech translation of *He Who Rides a Tiger.* Prague: Statni Nakladatelstvi Politicke, 1959.

Ken Tiike-rilla Ratsastta. Finnish translation of *He Who Rides a Tiger.* Kuopio: Kansankulttuuri Oy, 1957.

"Krokodyli Staw." Polish translation by Bohdan Gebarski of the short story "The Crocodile Pool," in *Adzanta: Nowele Indyjskie*, an anthology of Indian short stories. Warsaw: Pax, 1956.

Kto Raz Vysadol Na Tigra. Slovak translation of *He Who Rides a Tiger.* Bratislava: Slovenske Vydavatelstvo Krasnej, 1958.

Ladakh ki Chayya. Hindi translation by P. Machwe of *Shadow from Ladakh.* Delhi: Hind Pocket Books, 1970.

"Lattu Rams Abenteuer." German translation by Erica Kalmer of the short story "Lattu Ram Has an Adventure." Buenos Aires: *Argentinisches Tagblatt*, July 15, 1956; Zurich: *In freien Stunden*, Jan. 10, 1960; Bremen: *Bremer Nachrichten*, Jan. 21, 1959; Vienna: *Die Frau*, July 13, 1968; Cologne: *Welt der Arbeit*, April 24, 1970.

"Moment of Eternity, A." Bulgarian translation in *Septemvri* magazine, Sofia, 1958; reprinted in *Razkazi Ot Mnogo Meridiana* ("Short Stories from Many Meridians"). Sofia: Narodna Mladezh, 1967.

Musica para Mohini. Spanish translation of *Music for Mohini.* Barcelona: Editorial Vergara, 1963.
Musica per Mohini. Italian translation of *Music for Mohini.* Turin: S.A.I.E., 1955.
Musique pour Mohini. French translation of *Music for Mohini.* Paris: Le Club Français du Livre, 1952.
Muzika dl'a Mokhini. Perevod s angli'iskogo. Russian translation of *Music for Mohini.* Moscow: Moladai'ia Gvardiie, 1965.
Muzyka dla Mohini. Polish translation of *Music for Mohini.* Warsaw: Cqytelnik, 1963.
Pulissavarikkran. Malayalam translation by Chowallur Krishnankutty of *He Who Rides a Tiger.* Trichur: The Mangalodayam (Private) Ltd., 1963.
Qui Chevauche un Tigre. French translation of *He Who Rides a Tiger.* Paris: Calmann-Levy, 1956.
Sher Ke Sawar. Hindi translation by Shanta Jain of *He Who Rides a Tiger.* Bombay: Hindi Granth Ratnakar, 1958.
So Many Hungers! Translated by Chin-hsin Feng and K'ai-lan Kuo from Russian into Chinese. Peking: Tso Chia Ch'u Pan She, 1955.
So Many Hungers! Translations into Russian languages: by E. Kalashni kova, Moscow: Izd-vo Inostr. lit., 1949; into Georgian, Tbilisi: Sabchotta Sakarvelo, 1958; into Kazakh by S. Hajdarov, Alma-Alta: Kazakhstan State Lit. Publish., 1964; into Lithuanian by E. Kirmonajte, Vilnius: State Lit. Pub., 1956.
Sona. Hindi translation of *A Goddess Named Gold.* Delhi: Rajpal & Sons, 1973.
"Stadtbekannte Persönlichkeit." German translation by Erica Kalmer of the short story "Public Figure." Vienna: *Die Presse*, Sept. 23 1967; Berne: *Berner Tagblatt*, April 12, 1969; Linz: *Der gute Kamerad*, 1973.
Tak Wiele Jest Glodow. Polish translation of *So Many Hungers!* Warsaw: Ksiazka i Qiedza, 1951.
Tko Zajase Tigra. Serbo-Croatian translation of *He Who Rides a Tiger.* Zagreb: Zora, 1957.
Tolkova Mnogo Gladni. Bulgarian translation of *So Many Hungers!* Sofia: Izd. na Na Nation. Sivet na Otechestvenlia Front, 1958.
Triomf voor Mohini. Dutch translation of *Music for Mohini.* Den Haag: Ad. M. C. Stok, n.d.
"Un Momento di Eternità." Italian translation by Olga Ceretti Borsini of the short story "A Moment of Eternity," included in the anthology *World's Best.*
Una Diosa Llamada Oro. Spanish translation of *A Goddess Named Gold.* Barcelona: Editorial Vergara, 1960.
Velky Hlad. Slovak translation of *So Many Hungers!* Bratislava: Matica Slovenska, 1951.

Visappu! Visappu! Malayalam translation by Rosie Thomas of *So Many Hungers!* Kottayam: Sahitya Pravarthaka Coop., 1961.
Wer auf dem Tiger Reitet. German translation of *He Who Rides a Tiger.* Stuttgart: Gunther Verlag, 1957.
"Women in Revolt." Russian translation of short story in anthology. Moscow: State Publishing House of Fiction, 1952.

SECONDARY SOURCES

I. *General*

DE BARY, WM. THEODORE, ed. *Sources of Indian Tradition.* New York: Columbia University Press, 1964 (2 vol. text edition). Volume II provides a valuable cultural history of India from the opening of the sub-continent to the West in the late fifteenth century, through the struggle for and achievement of independence, to the post-partition period.

DERRETT, M. E. *The Modern Indian Novel in English, A Comparative Approach.* Brussels: Editions de l'Institut de Sociologie de l'Université Libre de Bruxelles, 1966.

EDWARDES, MICHAEL. *British India: 1772–1947.* New York: Taplinger Publishing Company, 1968. Background on the extent and sweeping effects of British rule in India.

————. *The West in Asia 1850–1914.* New York: G. P. Putnam's Sons, 1967. A survey history of imperialism and its effects in Asia. Maps and annotated bibliography.

JAIN, SUSHIL KUMAR. *Indian Literature in English.* Regina: University of Saskatchewan, 1965. A bibliography of poetry, drama, fiction, autobiography, and letters written by Indians in English, or translated from modern Indian languages into English.

JOSHI, VASANT. "Contemporary Indian Literature: 1950–1970." In *Literature East & West*, Vol. XV, No. 1, March 1971, pp. 38–54. Does not discuss Indian writers in English, but gives background on the historical and social conditions that have affected the approaches and themes of contemporary writers.

MCCUTCHION, DAVID. *Indian Writing in English.* Calcutta: Writers Workshop, 1969. A highly subjective selection and limited, though interesting, discussion of Indian poets and novelists writing in English.

MUGALI, R. S. "Nationalism and Cosmopolitanism in Literature: Indian Outlook." *Literature East & West*, Vol. IX, No. 2, Spring 1965, pp. 104–12. Traces from Vedic times to the present the long-standing interest of Indian writers in themes of nationalism, dwelling especially on the nineteenth and twentieth centuries.

NAIK, M. K. *et al.*, ed. *Critical Essays on Indian Writing in English*. Dharwar: Karnatak University, 1968. Essays by 28 writers. Of special interest are discussions of "India in Fiction," "The Language of Indian Fiction in English," and "Indo-English Literature."

NARASIMHAIAH, C. D. *The Swan and the Eagle*. Simla: Indian Institute of Advanced Study, 1969. A general discussion of English as a medium for Indian writers, with specific reference to five twentieth-century authors.

SPEAR, PERCIVAL. *A History of India*, Vol. II. Baltimore: Penguin Books, reprinted 1971. An excellent historical review from the coming of the Mughals (fourteenth century) to Nehru's India.

WHITE, JOANN, ed. *Impact! Asian Views of the West*. New York: Simon & Schuster, Inc., 1971. Collection of short pieces and excerpts from longer works reflecting the response of Asian writers to the impact of the West on their home cultures.

II. *Criticism*

ANAND, MULK RAJ. Review of *Towards Universal Man*. *Indian Literature*, Vol. IV, 1961, pp. 191–96.

ARCHER, ROSANNE. "Tragicomedy in India, 1947." *New York Herald Tribune Book Review*, Aug. 28, 1960. Review of *A Goddess Named Gold*.

BADAL, R. K. "Bhabani Bhattacharya and His Novels." *The Literary Half-Yearly*, Vol. XII, No. 2, July 1971, pp. 77–85.

BAKHTIYAR, IQBAL. "The Novel in Modern India." P.E.N. Bombay: All-India Centre, 1964.

BOYLE, F. A. Review of *He Who Rides a Tiger*. *Library Journal*, Sept. 15, 1954.

BRANDEL, SARAH ENSLEY. Review of *Shadow from Ladakh*. *Literature East & West*, Vol. XI, No. 2, June 1967, pp. 209–10.

CHANDRASEKHARAN, K. R. *Bhani Bhattacharya*. New Delhi: Arnold-Heine-mann, in association with the Humanities Press, New York, 1974. A monograph by the Director of the Language Institute, Gujarat University, Ahmedabad.

DERRETT, M. E. *The Modern Indian Novel in English: A Comparative Approach*. Brussels: Institut de Sociologie de l'Université Libre, 1966. References to Bhattacharya's first four novels; pp. 67–68, 101, 106, 120–23.

FISHER, MARLENE. "Personal and Social Change in Bhattacharya's Novels." *World Literature Written in English*, Vol. XII, No. 2, Nov. 1973, pp. 288–96.

———. "The Women in Bhattacharya's Novels." *World Literature Written in English*, Vol. XI, No. 1, April 1972, pp. 95–108.

GEROW, EDWIN. *Introduction to Indian Literature*. Chicago: University of Chicago Press, 1974. Especially helpful for its discussion of some of the esthetic measurements of Indian Literature, including reference to *He Who Rides a Tiger*.

GUIDRY, FREDERICK. Review of *A Goddess Named Gold* in *The Christian Science Monitor*, Sept. 8, 1960.

HITREC, JOSEPH. "Indian Pathfinder." A review of *He Who Rides a Tiger* in *The Saturday Review*, Nov. 20, 1954.

——. "Magic Alone Could Not Do the Trick." A review of *A Goddess Named Gold* in *The New York Times Book Review*, Aug. 21, 1960.

Indian Literature. Vol. XIII, No. 3, 1970. Review of *Contemporary Indian Short Stories*, Series II, edited by Bhattacharya.

IYENGAR, K. R. SRINIVASA. "The Contemporary Indian Short Story." *Indian Literature*, Vol. XIII, No. 3, 1970, pp. 36–44.

——. *Indian Writing in English*. Bombay: Asia Publishing House, 1962. Includes references to Bhattacharya, with some historical background on the first four novels, pp. 237, 325–31, 338.

LASK, THOMAS. "Rolling Mills and Hunger Strikes." A review of *Shadow from Ladakh* in *The New York Times*, June 1, 1966.

LE ROY, DAVID J. "Evil as Portrayed in Five Indian Novels." *Thought*, May 12, 1962.

Mahfil: A Quarterly of South Asian Literature (now entitled *Journal of South Asian Literature*). Interview with Bhabani Bhattacharya, Vol. V, Nos. 1 & 2, 1968–69, pp. 43–48.

MEHTA, P. P. *Indo-Anglian Fiction: An Assessment*. Bareilly: Prakash Book Depot, 1968. Discusses Bhattacharya's first five novels chiefly as examples of the "Rural Novel" and the "Social Novel," pp. 248–52, 278–79.

MUKHERJEE, MEENAKSHI. *The Twice-Born Fiction*. Delhi: Heinemann, 1971.

MUKHERJEE, SUJIT. References to Bhattacharya in "The Indo-Anglian Novelist as Best Seller," *Literature East & West*, Vol. XIII, Nos. 1 & 2, June 1969, pp. 83–93.

NANDAKUMAR, PREMA. "The Achievement of the Indo-Anglian Novelist." *The Literary Criterion*, Vol. VI, No. 1, Winter 1961.

——. "The Amulet Gandhiji Gave." Review of *A Goddess Named Gold* in *Swarajya*, July 28, 1962.

——. "English Writing by Indians: Another Rich Year." *Indian Literature*, Vol. XI, No. 4, 1968, pp. 19–37. Mentions *Shadow from Ladakh*.

——. "Indian Writing in English." *Indian Literature*, Vol. III, No. 1, Oct. 1959–March 1960, pp. 52–55. Mentions *He Who Rides a Tiger*.

——. "Indian Writing in English: A Growingly Significant Literature." *Indian Literature*, Vol. XII, No. 4, 1969, pp. 39–49. Includes discussion of *Shadow from Ladakh*, *Steel Hawk*, and *Contemporary Indian Short Stories*, Series II, edited by Bhattacharya.

NARASIMHAIAH, C. D. "Indian Writing in English—An Introduction." *Journal of Commonwealth Literature*, No. 5, July 1968.

PARTON, MARGARET. "He Rode a Lie as If It Were a Tiger." Review of *He*

Who Rides a Tiger in *The Herald Tribune Book Review*, Oct. 24, 1954.

PAYNE, ROBERT. Review of *He Who Rides a Tiger*. The *New York Times*, Oct. 24, 1954.

PRESCOTT, ORVILLE. Review of *He Who Rides a Tiger* in "Books of the Times." The *New York Times*, Dec. 28, 1954.

RAJAN, B. "The Indian Virtue." *Journal of Commonwealth Literature*, No. 1, Sept. 1965.

RAO, B. SYAMALA. "Bhabani Bhattacharya as a Novelist." *Triveni, Journal of Indian Renaissance*, Vol. XL, No. 1, April 1971, pp. 35–40.

RAY, LILA. "Bhabani Bhattacharya: A Profile." *Indian Literature*, Vol. XI, No. 2, April–July, 1968, pp. 73–76.

"Rural World of Bhabani." *Enlite: The National Magazine* (Baroda), Sept. 14, 1968, pp. 27–30. A concise survey of the author's achievements, his brief diplomatic career, and a discussion of his "humanistic philosophy."

SHARPE, PATRICIA L. Review of *Shadow from Ladakh* in *Mahfil: A Quarterly of South Asian Literature* (now entitled *Journal of South Asian Literature*), Vol. V, Nos. 1 & 2, 1968–69, pp. 134–39.

SHIMER, DOROTHY BLAIR. "Bhabani Bhattacharya—Gandhi Biographer." *The Journal of Indian Writing in English*, Vol. II, No. 2, July 1974.

SINGH, R. S. "Bhabani Bhattacharya: A Novelist of Dreamy Wisdom." *The Banasthali Patrika*, No. 13.

SWEENY, MARY K. "More Than Glitter." *America*, Oct. 8, 1960. Review of *A Goddess Named Gold*.

TARINAYA, M. "Bhabani Bhattacharya's *So Many Hungers!*" *Indian Literature of the Past Fifty Years*, Mysore Golden Jubilee Volume, C. D. Narasimhaiah, ed.

TOWLE, LAWRENCE. "A Changing World." *The Courant Magazine*, Aug. 21, 1966. Review of *Shadow from Ladakh*.

VERGHESE, PAUL C. "Indian English and Man in Indo-Anglian Fiction." *Indian Literature*, Vol. XIII, No. 1, March 1970.

———. *Problems of the Creative Indian Writer in English*. Bombay: Somaiya Publications, 1971.

WOOD, PERCY. "Story of an Indian Village the Best in Years." *The Chicago Tribune*, Sept. 25, 1960. Review of *A Goddess Named Gold*.

Index

147